68-8313

For Julia, Sebastian and Dolly

Library of Congress Catalog card number
68-8313

Henry Spencer Moore

I wonder whether putting in Spencer makes
my name into somebody not quite known to me.
I have never used the name Spencer
since I was a boy at the Grammar School.

1898	Born at Castleford, Yorkshire, 30th July.
1910	Won scholarship to Castleford Grammar School.
1917	Joined 15th London Regiment (Civil Service Rifles). Gassed at Cambrai. Sent back to England, December.
1919	Demobilised in February. Entered Leeds School of Art.
1921	Won Royal Exhibition Scholarship in Sculpture. Entered Royal College of Art
1924	Awarded Royal College of Art travelling scholarship, but on completing third year as student, appointed instructor in the sculpture school for seven years.
1928	First one-man exhibition at Warren Gallery. Received first public commission—a relief for the facade of the new Underground Building, St James's, London.
1929	Married Irina Radetzsky.
1932	Moved to Chelsea School of Art to establish department of sculpture.
1940	Began shelter drawings. Appointed official War artist. After studio damaged by bombing in October took house at Much Hadham, Hertfordshire, where he has lived ever since.
1941	Appointed a Trustee of Tate Gallery for seven years.
1943	Madonna and Child commissioned for St Matthew's Church, Northampton.
1946	Birth of his daughter, Mary. Visited New York for first major retrospective exhibition at Museum of Modern Art.
1948	Awarded International Sculpture prize, 24th Venice Biennale.
1949	Reappointed a Trustee of Tate Gallery for a further seven years.
1953	Awarded International Prize for sculpture, 2nd Sao Paulo Biennale. Visited Brazil and Mexico.
1955	Elected Honorary Member of American Academy of Arts and Sciences. Appointed a Trustee of National Gallery. Appointed member of the Order of the Companions of Honour.
1958	Created Honorary Doctor of Arts by Harvard University. Awarded second Sculpture Prize, Carnegie International, Pittsburgh.
1959	Created Honorary Doctor of Laws by University of Cambridge. Awarded International Sculpture Prize, Tokyo Biennale.
1961	Elected Honorary Member of American Academy of Arts and Letters. Created Honorary Doctor of Literature by University of Oxford. Elected a Member of the Academie der Kunste, Berlin.
1962	Created Honorary Doctor of Engineering by Technische Hochschule, Berlin. Made Honorary Freeman of the Borough of Castleford, Yorkshire. Sculpture commissioned for Lincoln Center, New York. Elected Honorary Fellow of Lincoln College, Oxford.
1963	Awarded Antonio Feltrinelli Prize for Sculpture by Accademia dei Lincei, Rome. Appointed Member of the Order of Merit.
1964	Awarded Fine Arts Medal by Institute of Architects for the United States. Appointed Member of Arts Council of Great Britain.
1965	Elected Honorary Fellow of Churchill College, Cambridge.
1966	Created Honorary Doctor of Fine Arts by Yale University. Elected a Fellow of British Academy.
1967	Created Honorary Doctor of Laws by St Andrews University, Scotland. Created Honorary Doctor of Arts by Royal College of Art, London.
1968	Awarded Erasmus Prize, Holland. Awarded Einstein Memorial Prize, U.S.A.

Photographed and edited by

John Hedgecoe

Words by

Henry Moore

Simon and Schuster / New York

Introduction

Looking at this book and the different periods of my life that it covers, I'm surprised, for one thing, that I have done so much sculpture. And although the book doesn't include everything that I have done, I'm reminded of the intensity that went into my work at so many different periods, and of the many often purely physical sculptural problems I had to overcome.

I would like to think that some of this energy has become imprisoned in my work so that other people can feel it.

All the artists that I admire—Rubens, Michelangelo, Tintoretto, Rembrandt, Rodin and some others—have a life-giving power in their work.

Landscape has been for me one of the sources of this energy. It is generally thought that no sculptor is much interested in landscape, but is only concerned with the solid, immediate form of the human figure or animals. For myself, I have always been very interested in landscape. (I can never read on a train —I have to look out of the window in case I miss something.) As well as landscape views and cloud formations, I find that all natural forms are a source of unending interest—tree trunks, the growth of branches from the trunk, each finding its individual air-space, the texture and variety of grasses, the shape of shells, of pebbles, etc. The whole of Nature is an endless demonstration of shape and form, and it surprises me when artists try to escape from this. Not to look at and to use Nature in one's work is unnatural to me.

I have no inhibitions about using different forms and different experiences combined together in one work, whether their source is animal, human, or from natural materials.

By the intense study of numerous particular examples in Nature, one can discover certain underlying principles which can be used, singly or combined, to produce a new and unique work which owes its unity to the artist's instinctive comprehension of laws of Nature.

The whole basis of my reaction to form and my understanding of it is fundamentally related to the human body and to my own physical experiences. For me this is reality.

I think that one of the most important things about this book is that as a result of the long period over which John Hedgecoe has been taking the photographs, as well as through all the communication we have had together, he has learnt what I'm aiming at in sculpture, and has been able to reveal and give added meaning and interest to it.

Henry Moore

As a small boy these slag heaps seemed much larger than the Pyramids

. . I mean they had as big a monumentality as any mountain, in fact perhaps more. Monumentality has always been important to me although at first I wasn't conscious of it. It was only later when I came to think about sculpture that I tried to analyse it. Some works of art have it and others don't. It's almost impossible to define. It's really a matter of scale. The Cézanne bathers are monumental. I have a small Cézanne that could be enlarged to ten or twenty times its original size and it would still have great monumentality. Few other painters have the same sense of scale. I wouldn't say, for instance, that Watteau, though I think he is a great artist, has the monumentality of Rubens although Watteau was greatly influenced by Rubens.

A coal hole cover in Roundhill Road, Castleford, where I was born.

Roundhill Road with the pit heap in the background. I wonder
whether the place has changed at all. The people look just the
same as they always did; that wide stance on a solid base, very
firm on the earth.

Number 30 Roundhill Road. Downstairs my father had his political meetings. My bedroom was on the other side.

My mother + father

Me — at 11 yrs.
(at C.G.S.)
Selth 1909.

tch + chain?

Around this time is when
I heard my Sunday School
Teacher tell about the
Great sculptor Michelangelo — which made
me say that when I grew up I was
going to be a great sculptor

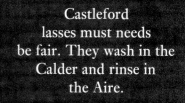

Castleford
lasses must needs
be fair. They wash in the
Calder and rinse in
the Aire.

My first bit of wood carving of a serious nature, using proper tools; I had only done wood carving with a penknife before. I must have been sixteen or seventeen at the time. The war had been on a year or so, and former students were being wounded and killed. I carved this memorial for them. Miss Gostick, who was the art teacher at the school, provided me with the tools and showed me how to use them.

Methley Church, about two miles from Castleford. It contains the first real sculptures that I remember.

I was very impressed by these recumbent effigy figures, particularly by the simplicity of the woman's head. The female figure is always more simple than the male, less muscles and wrinkles. It was this and the almost Egyptian stillness of the figure that appealed to me, as well as the hands coming away from the body.

I have always thought Rievaulx Abbey to be a most impressive monument. In its present state it is more sculpture than architecture. When architecture is unusable it inevitably becomes aesthetically the same as sculpture. This is perhaps why I like ruins. For example, the Parthenon. Now that the light passes through it, it is far more sculptural than if it were all filled in.

As boys we used to play in the clay pits belonging to Castleford Pottery, and make sculptures with the clay. It was so beautifully malleable. At evening school pots and plates were provided for us to decorate. Miss Gostick is on my left.

An early drawing of mine. Very Beardsley. There were three of us, Dalby, Wainwright and myself, all roughly the same age, competing for any art jobs that might be going in the Grammar School, like designing the cover of the school magazine, or costumes for the school concert. Wainwright, who was the most precocious, introduced me to this kind of Beardsley black and white technique.

I designed this cover for a play I wrote. They used to call me Harry then. I went through periods of first being called Henry, then Harry and then Hal. All the time I preferred Henry, but other people would insist on making variations. Now I can date my friends. When they call me Harry, I know I haven't seen them for thirty years.

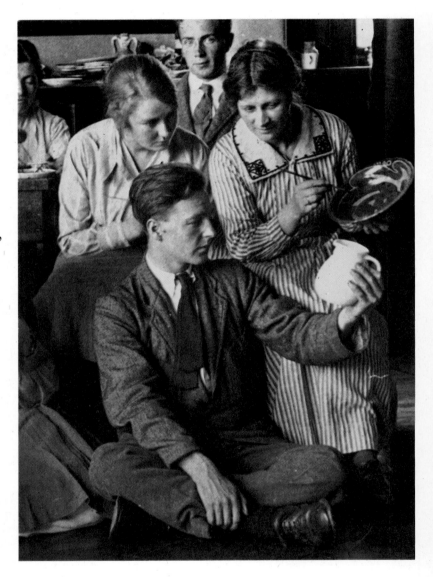

NARAYANA AND BHATARYAN

A PLAY ~ BY HARRY SPENCER MOORE

December 1919.
Castleford Grammar School Pottery Class
for staff + old students.
in front row
H.M. Arthur Dalby
+ Raymond
Coxon.

Alice Gostick

R.C.A Picnic on Thames.
me + Raymond Coxon
with paddles.

me, pale + frail
on sick leave
after being gassed
at Cambrai.

Taken in the
Fives - Court
at Castleford
Grammar
School.

Spring 1918.

Jug decorated
in Pottery Class.
1919 or 1920

Me at 18 —
just joined - up.

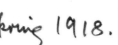

30

H.M. & Raymond Coxon

me & Barry Hart

Photograph taken by Edwin Smith

Middle picture – Chelsea Art School
Christmas show
me as Archaic Greek Torso.
Robert Medley on left – Raymond
Coxon on right

Irina at 8 yrs.
taken in the Crimea
Russia.

Honey Pot by me.
↓

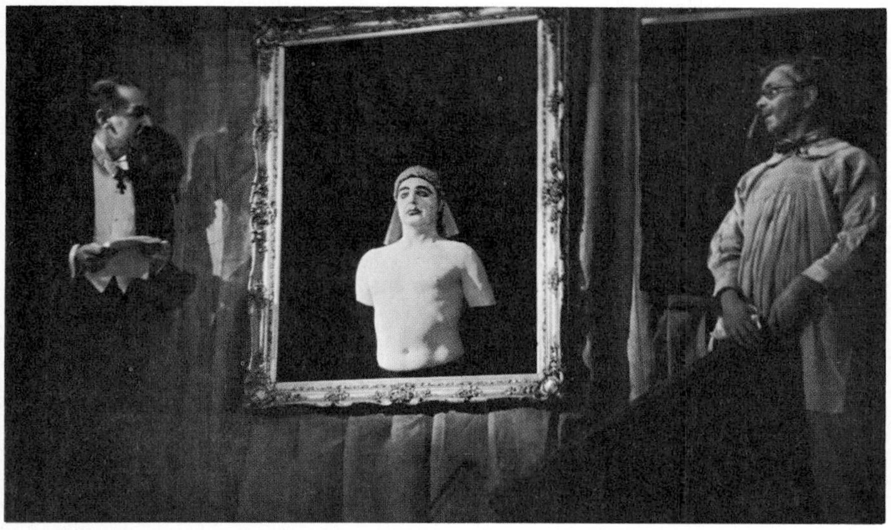

My mother
at her house
in Kent.

My platoon in Civil Service Rifles.
1917.
Winchester.

→ me

Irina at 6 yrs – taken Caucasus – Russia.
my ~~favourite~~
favourite portrait of her – just like Mary at 6 yrs.

31

My father was very sensible and although he did not know much about the art world, he knew enough to realise that an artist's life was likely to be an awful struggle. And so, when I was fourteen or fifteen, he advised me to carry on with my education and become a qualified teacher like my brothers and sisters. His point was that, after I had an assured living, I could then paint or do the sculpture that I wanted. I would still advise art students to follow that advice today, as only one in a thousand is likely to become a really good artist.

After passing School Certificate, which meant I could have gone to Leeds University or a Teachers' Training College, I became a student teacher at my old elementary school. It was in 1915 and because of the war they were so short of teachers that I didn't get much time for my general studies. In fact I was virtually a full time teacher.

The calling up age for the Army was eighteen and a half, at which stage you could be posted to any regiment, although usually it would be your local one. In my case that would have been the Yorkshire Light Infantry. My father, who was always thinking of his children's future, said, "I think, Henry, you ought to try to choose a regiment rather than just be posted wherever they want to send you." And since I was very keen and very patriotic I agreed to volunteer before being called up.

My first choice was the Artists' Rifles because, since I wanted to be an artist, I thought this would give me some of the right atmosphere. My second choice was The Honourable Artillery Company, which some student friends of mine had joined. My third choice was the Civil Service Rifles, the 15th London Regiment. My father sent me down to London to apply to these different regiments. The Artists' Rifles had a

waiting list. So did the H.A.C., but the Civil Service Rifles had a few vacancies and they took me. It must have been about February 1917, although it might have been a bit earlier. I think my father was right, because it meant that I was with a different set of people than I would have been in the local Yorkshire regiment.

After the war ended, I was one of the first in my battalion to be demobilised because the Government decided that it was more important for students, teachers and certain other professions to get back to civilian life before the rest. In fact I was in the first batch of ten to be released. We were played down to the station by the Regimental Band. There was great jubilation that we had reached the stage where people were actually going home.

I arrived home in February 1919 and straight away I applied for an Army grant. The Government had brought in a scheme for helping students, whose careers had been interrupted, to return to their studies. Fortunately this scheme was applicable to me and Miss Gostick had got hold of all the forms that I had to fill in. Knowing I wanted to be a sculptor and not a teacher, and since I was then two years older, my father waived his common sense objections and I applied to go to Leeds School of Art.

After my month's demobilisation leave I learnt that I had been accepted, but that I must wait for six months. There was still a great shortage of teachers and so, to fill in the time, I went back and taught in the elementary school at Castleford. But, three nights a week, I went to Leeds School of Art for evening classes, so that I wouldn't arrive absolutely raw as a full time student in September.

I hadn't enjoyed my time as a student teacher in 1915 because

The very first stone carving I ever did. It must have been in the Christmas holidays of 1921-2. I recently discovered it in my garage amongst some boxes of pebbles that I have had for over forty years. It's a Mother and Child and it's made in Cornish Serpentine, which is quite a hard stone. You can see that I didn't finish it. It was too tough and too small to hold, being only four and a half inches high.

as a boy of seventeen I found the miners' children very rough. There was one time when, because I had kept them in at playtime for some misdemeanour or other, they waited round the corner of the school buildings ready to throw stones at me as I left school at the end of the day. However, when I came out of the army, having been a physical training instructor, it was very different. I had complete and absolute control, for I had learnt how to cope with the problems of discipline.

I spent my first year at Leeds taking the drawing examination and, the following year, I asked the Principal, a person named Hayward Ryder, if I could take the Board of Education's examination in sculpture. It created a bit of difficulty because, since there wasn't a sculpture school, they had to set one up. They appointed a sculpture teacher, called Cotterill, who had just come down from the Royal College of Art. He had been in the Army before that, and so he was probably twenty-six or twenty-seven. For a whole year, I was Cotterill's only full-time student, and he looked after me like a child. He was always breathing down my neck, but, in a way, this was a help because I got through the two-year course in one year, as well as winning a Royal Exhibition, which was at that time the only way of getting into the Royal College of Art. Cotterill was an intelligent person, and a good teacher. He did have part-time students, and even classes, but I was his one real care. Later, he became Head of York School of Art.

Sadly my father died in 1922, when I'd only just begun sculpture. My mother had no knowledge of art. Like many parents, she thought that whatever I did was jolly good. That was her attitude, except that one day I remember her saying, while she was watching me carving a big piece of stone, that she wondered why, when I'd been to Grammar School, I should have chosen such a hard physical job. She felt that if one could avoid sweating at manual work, one should do so! At the Royal College of Art, where I arrived in 1921, the stone carving instructor was Barry Hart. He was almost the same age as I was, and had been appointed to teach the art of carving purely and simply because his family were professional stone carvers. They were not sculptors, but they could, by using pointing machines, copy sculpture. The Royal Academicians would send them the plaster cast of a highly finished realistic portrait bust which had first been modelled in clay with eyebrows, eye lashes and nostrils in detail. This type of work demanded the precise use of a pointing machine which would take measurements to within one thousandth of an inch. This procedure was, of course, one of the reasons why the work of the Royal Academy was so uninspired and dead. Had we students been allowed to carve more freely there might have been more quality of stone about our work. Derwent Wood was a Royal Academician and Head of the Sculpture Department of the Royal College. He believed that it was impossible to produce an absolutely correct copy of an existing model for sculpture without using a pointing machine, and since an identical copy was what he wanted, we were only taught how to carve in that way. We were given classical sculptures to copy and no original carving was permitted. I believed that I could copy faithfully without using the pointing machine and I persuaded Barry Hart to let me try to carve my piece freely. Although he himself could handle a hammer and chisel remarkably well, he still didn't believe it was possible and I had to make false points in pencil on the marble so that, when Derwent Wood came round, he would think I was using the pointing machine.

The School of Sculpture at the Royal College of Art about 1900.

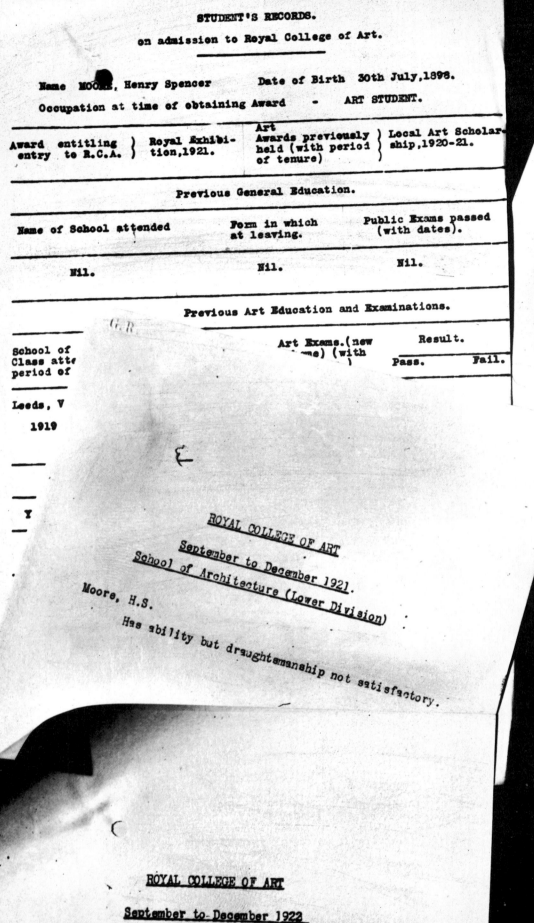

STUDENT'S RECORDS.

on admission to Royal College of Art.

Name MOORE, Henry Spencer   Date of Birth 30th July, 1898.

Occupation at time of obtaining Award   -   ART STUDENT.

Award entitling entry to R.C.A.	Royal Exhibition, 1921.	Art Awards previously held (with period of tenure)	Local Art Scholarship, 1920-21.

Previous General Education.

Name of School attended	Form in which at leaving.	Public Exams passed (with dates).
Nil.	Nil.	Nil.

Previous Art Education and Examinations.

School of Class atte period of		Art Exams.(new me) (with	Result.	
			Pass.	Fail.
Leeds, V 1919				

ROYAL COLLEGE OF ART

September to December 1921.

School of Architecture (Lower Division)

Moore, H.S.

Has ability but draughtsmanship not satisfactory.

ROYAL COLLEGE OF ART

September to December 1922

School of Sculpture (Upper Division)

Moore, H.S.

Is a good student who shows great improvement in all sections, his carving is excellent, drawing very promising.

ROYAL CO

Period endi

Moore,

School of Modelling

His life work shows improvemen
my liking. Is much interested in ce

(Sgd.) F.Derwent
26. 6. 2

ROYAL COLLEGE OF AR

September to December,

Modelling School

Moore, H.S.

This student shows great im
His drawings are excellent
improvement   He appears
his interest of tradition

ROYAL COLLEGE

Jan.
April to July

School of Sculpture (

Moore, H.S.

Marked improvement i

OF ART.

1922

Division.

sign not to

ROYAL COLLEGE OF ART.

_____

SCHOOLS ASSOCIATESHIP TEST, 1923.

_____

Number I. A.

Name in full _Henry Spencer Moore._

School specialised in _Sculpture_

(1905—1906) Wt. 6227—B 6127 500 5/15 R.C.&S. 128

Pass.

ent in his life work.
his design might show
somewhat limited in
pture.

ROYAL COLLEGE OF ART

School of Sculpture

January to July 1924.

Moore, H.S.

Has shown great improvement in all branches, hard working,
his life work shows marked promise, altogether a good
student.

ivision)

work and design.

The first two of these sculptures are College works. Nothing else here was done in College. It would not have been allowed. I did the rest in the digs I shared with Raymond Coxon in Walham Green. I couldn't do stone carvings in my digs because of the dust and chips, but wood carving was all right because I could clear up afterwards.

Part of my student studies were animals in action, and usually I would choose a horse. I have always liked the shape of horses, although, apart from this little bronze horse, I haven't used them much in my sculpture.

The first sculptures I sold were two wood carvings to Sir William Rothenstein's brother, Charles. They fetched £7 and £10, which was quite a lot in those days. My scholarship, while a student at the College, was £90 a year, and so, compared with the other students, I was relatively rich.

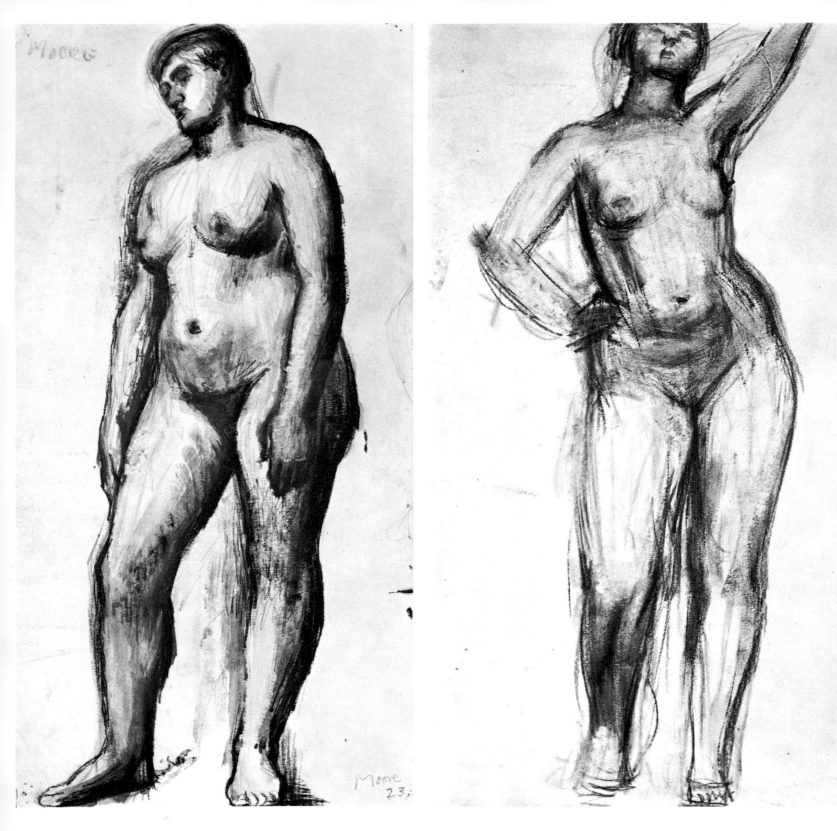

I am very satisfied with these life drawings. I spent two years at Leeds School of Art and four years at the Royal College of Art doing three or four days a week of modelling or drawing from life, trying to understand the figure. Afterwards I had seven years teaching life drawing and modelling at the Royal College and another seven years teaching it at Chelsea Art School. When I was looking at students' work I found I had to look perhaps even more intensely than at my own work. So altogether I had twenty years of continually concentrated observation and attempt at understanding the human figure.

The pure outline is a shorthand method of drawing. This is how Matisse drew at the end of his life and also Picasso. But they began their careers with this kind of highly finished three-dimensional drawing using light and shade, and then later in life simplified their styles. This is the real way to understand things.

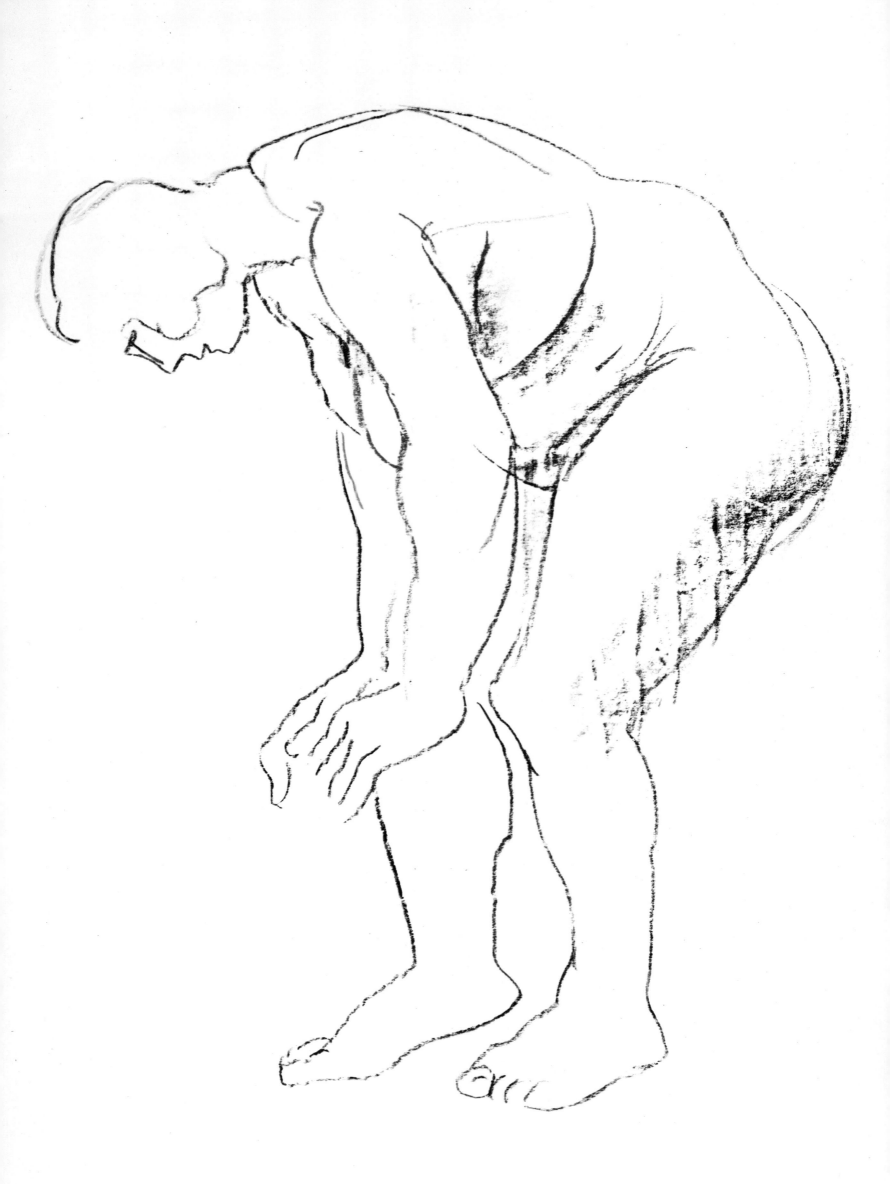

Paris.
May 27ᵗʰ

Dear Mr Wellington. About a fortnight ago I got poisoning into a cut in my hand — It was progressing favourably until three or four days ago when it began to trouble me again & to day I am seriously concerned about it & think it needs careful attention, & so I have decided to return home to Norfolk immediately where I can consult my own doctor.

However as I said in my last letter that you could count on me making the Scholarship last until the middle of June, I shall if my hand is better by then return here about the 10th of June & shall be able to remain roughly a fortnight — & returning to College some few days before the end of June — Should you have any cause to write me my home address is — 2 Church Street — Wells — Norfolk.

Thank you for your last letter & for the speeding of the arrival of the last instalment of the scholarship. —

yrs sincerely,
Henry Moore

My goodness, I was thankful to receive the instalment referred to in this letter. The reason was that I had arrived in Venice expecting it to be there and I had almost no money left. I was taken by gondola from the train to a hotel on the Lido. I had no idea that the Lido was one of the most expensive parts of Venice. After one day I asked how much my room cost and discovered I hadn't enough money to pay for it. I couldn't leave so I sent urgent letters to Wellington, the Registrar, and just hung on. In those days letter post was not as quick as it is now because there was no air mail. I was there for about a fortnight and all the time the bill was mounting up. As a result I didn't really enjoy Venice—not half as much as I could have done.

25
—— R.C.A.
223

29th May, 1925.

My dear Moore,

I am very sorry to hear from your letter this morning that you have got poisoning in the hand. It is not always easy to get in touch with good medical advice when abroad though there is no doubt that attention and skill of the highest order can be found in Paris. At any rate I hope your own doctor and a change of air will put you all right, and that you will be able to carry out your programme. I shall be glad to know how you are.

Yours sincerely,

Henry Moore, Esq.,
2, Church Street,
Wells,
Norfolk.

42

I began believing in direct stone carving, in being true to the material by not making stone look like flesh or making wood behave like metal. This is the tenet that I took over from sculptors like Brancusi and Modigliani. It made me hesitate to make the material do what I wanted until I began to realise this was a limitation in sculpture so that often the forms were all buried inside each other and heads were given no necks. As a result you will find that in some of my early work there is no neck simply because I was frightened to weaken the stone. Out of an exaggerated respect for the material, I was reducing the power of the form.

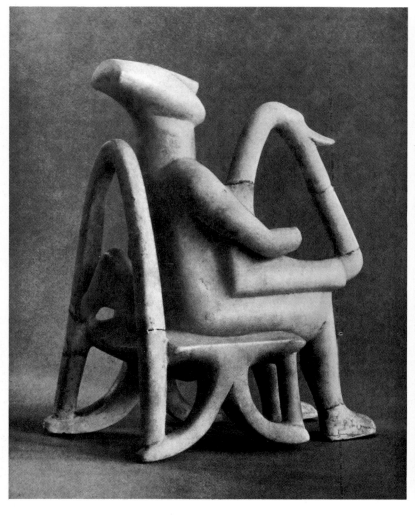

Then I became aware that in some examples of primitive art, the sculptor had been bold enough to make three-dimensional form out of a solid block, and it gave me courage to do it in my own sculpture. I found it very surprising that they had dared to make the necks as long as they had. Some of their carvings are so thin from the side that often you find them broken. Their vision had not been restricted by their material, and certainly some of the little figures of Cycladic times are remarkable examples of early sculptors being so concerned with realising their sculptural ideas that they had taken greater liberties with the material than I had thought were possible.

All the time I had this desire to achieve complete form and reality in my work.

48

Number 3 Grove Studios, Hammersmith. The photograph must have been taken in 1925 or 1926, because it has in it a figure that I never finished. A number of the others later got broken. I just didn't take care of them. I've never purposely set about destroying any of my sculptures, although I have destroyed drawings. I remember once looking through some drawings with Irina, thinking some of them were rather poor, and beginning to tear them up. I held each one up and asked her what she thought. I might say, "I don't think it's good," and she might say, "Oh no, keep that." Then I might say of another one, "I think this is not so bad," and she would say, "No, I don't like that, that can go." Between us we got worked up into a frenzy, because there is great pleasure in destruction especially in tearing up a thing you have done; tearing it in half. We ended up with a pile on the studio floor. We must have destroyed a thousand drawings. It was good for the spirit.

I had been away for four months in 1924 on a travelling scholarship and I had been looking at things from an entirely different point of view than before. When I came back, I found it terribly difficult to finish the sculptures that I had been working on before I left. The figure that I am working on is of a rather distraught and dramatic woman.

There is a big arm, nearly eleven feet long, in the British Museum, which impressed me. It's Egyptian. It has a kind of squareness about it which I found interesting. It is not that I imitated it consciously, it's just that, if something impresses you, you can't help being influenced by it. This happens to every artist. It is only the great artists who can emerge from these influences and create their own individual style.

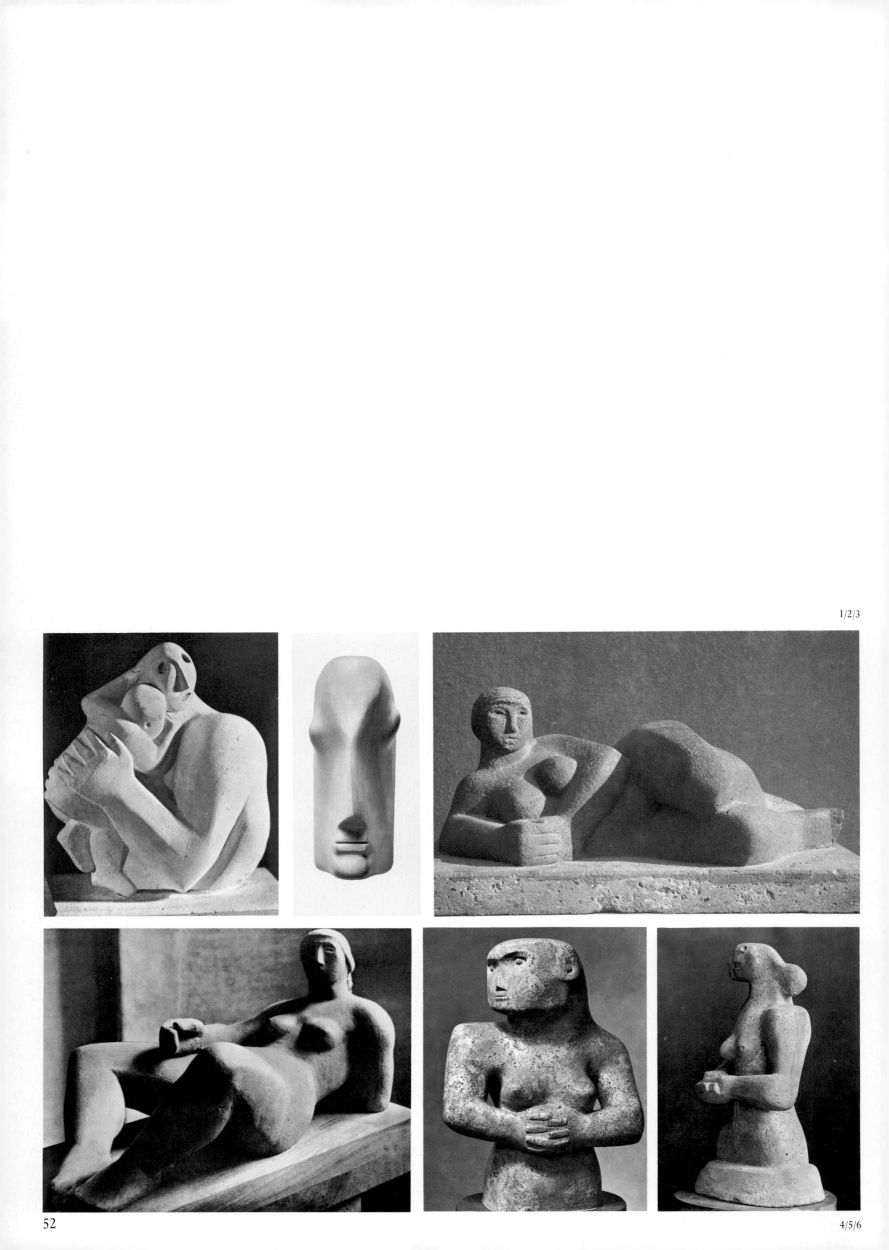

This was the period when I had slight cubist tendencies, and in the square form of the Mother and Child some of this influence shows. The whole rhythm of this reclining figure is a right-angled rhythm.

7

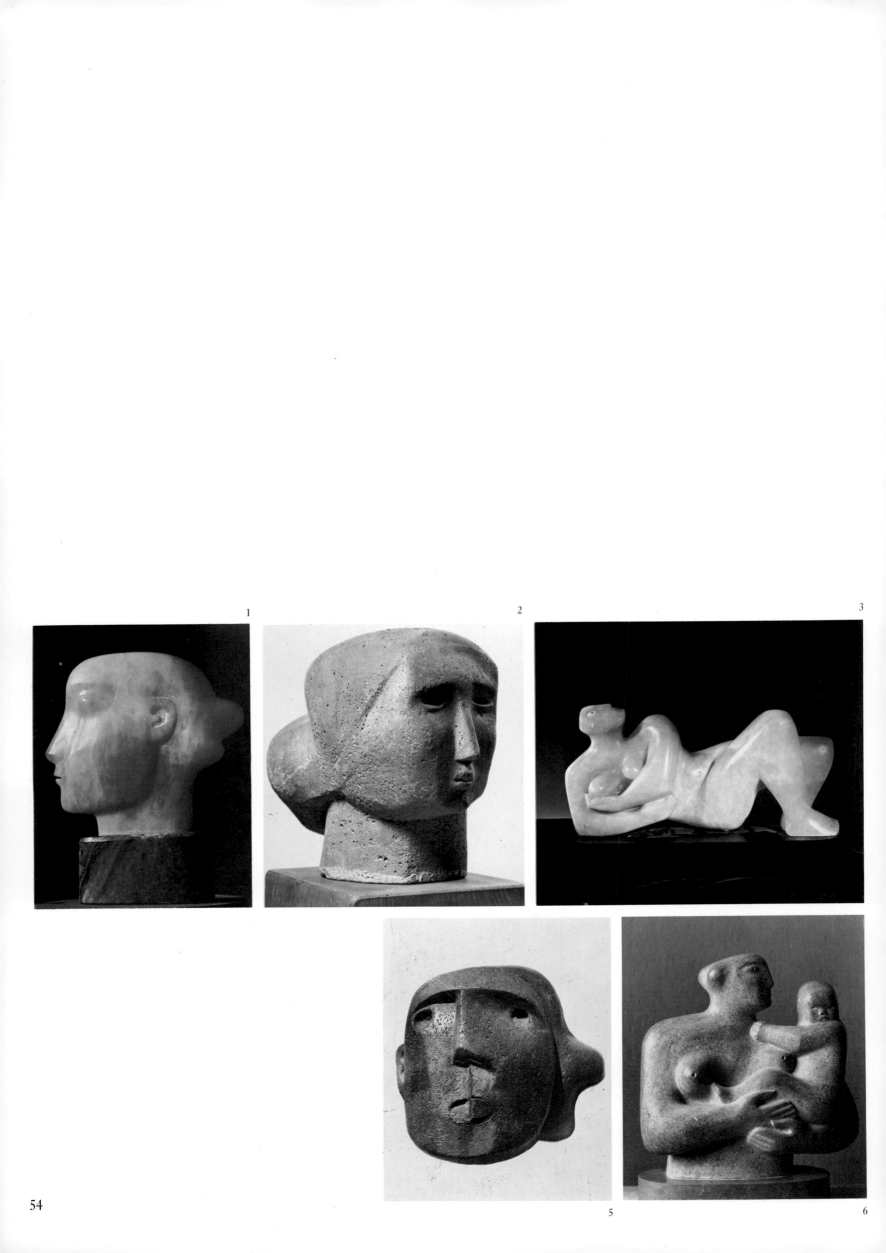

I've always had a liking for squareness. The squareness of a right angle is a very vigorous action. This may be one reason why I appreciate Mexican and particularly Aztec sculpture.

4

7

Masks isolate the facial expression, enabling you to concentrate on the face alone. They have, of course, been used throughout history, particularly as theatrical devices. Although the back of the head can be as beautiful and as interesting to a sculptor, it can't be as expressive, in the ordinary sense of the word, as the face.

Perhaps I have done six or seven masks in all. The first one in 1924 was definitely of Mexican influence, after seeing and admiring the Mexican masks in the British Museum.

In this mask I wanted to give the eyes tremendous penetration and to make them stare, because it is the eyes which most easily express human emotion. In other masks, I used the asymmetrical principle in which one eye is quite different from the other, and the mouth is at an angle bringing back the balance.

I had noticed this in some of the Mexican masks, and I began to find it in reality in all faces.

And as I began to find out that, in Nature, living things, because of the effect of their environment, are never perfectly symmetrical, this principle became fundamental to my work. You will find in everybody's face that one eye is different from the other, or the mouth is not quite horizontal, or one nostril is a little higher than the other, or the forehead comes out a little further on one side than the other.

And it is when you come to look at a person's face with acute observation that you will find these many small variations that make all the difference between a really sensitive portrait and a dull one.

The great advantage of sculpture is its three-dimensionality and that it can be seen from innumerable different angles. I prefer asymmetrical sculpture to the perfectly symmetrical because, in a symmetrical work, since one side is identical to the other, it can have only half the different viewpoints of an asymmetrical work.

Then there are the environmental influences, such as wind, sun, sea or even disease, which inevitably work against perfect symmetry in Nature.

And so it is that, throughout life, the principle of balance controls Nature's asymmetry.

56

These are about 1928, when I was experimenting with cement. At the time reinforced concrete was the new material for architecture. As I have always been interested in materials, I thought I ought to learn about the use of concrete for sculpture in case I ever wanted to connect a piece of sculpture with a concrete building. The first method of using concrete I tried, was building it up on an armature and then rubbing it down after it had set. This I had to do very quickly because the cement and the gritty aggregate mixed with it set so hard that all my tools used to wear out. Secondly, I tried casting in concrete.

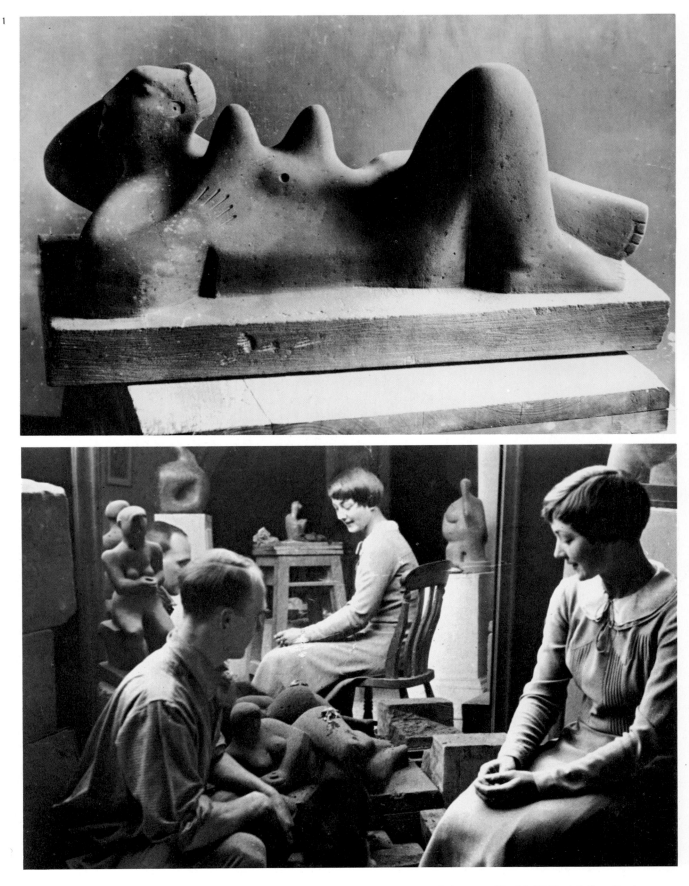

1

A corner of the 11a Parkhill Road Studio into which Irina and I moved after coming back from our honeymoon in Devon. My time at 11a was a tremendously intense period for me.

From very early on I have had an obsession with
the Mother and Child theme. It has been a
universal theme from the beginning of time and
some of the earliest sculptures we've found from the
Neolithic Age are of a Mother and Child. I discovered,
when drawing, I could turn every little scribble, blot
or smudge into a Mother and Child. (Later on, I
did the same with the Reclining Figure theme!) So
that I was conditioned, as it were, to see it in
everything. I suppose it could be explained as a
"Mother" complex.

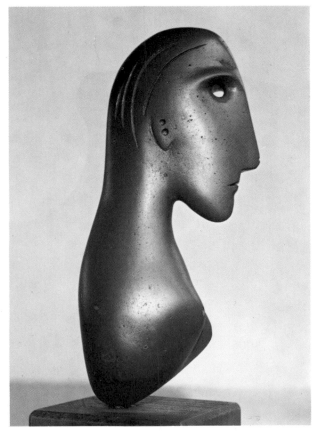

The year 1931 was very important for me
because I became more conscious of forcing forms
in depth. It is easy to carve both sides of a
sculpture but I had a real desire to make three-
dimensional form by thinking of it also from
within, and not only as a solid object like a tree
trunk. The division between the breasts and
the hands, even going right through to the
other side of this girl figure, was the beginning
of the "hole" period for me. I had used holes
before, in 1928, making an eye that goes right
through the head of the sculpture, but not for
a three-dimensional form reason.

We all think we see three-dimensional form—but we don't. People have to be trained to comprehend spaces in order to understand the shape of something. Great draughtsmen such as Rembrandt, Michelangelo or Rubens could each draw three-dimensional form. Rembrandt in his late self portraits could make the nose have the right projection in front of the cheeks, and the forehead the right distance in front of the eyes. He could do this to a great extent as a young man, but he did it better and better as he got older. Now if a genius takes all that time to see form and to learn how to represent it completely, the average person cannot expect to understand it fully. He may get a general idea, but no more.

1

2/3

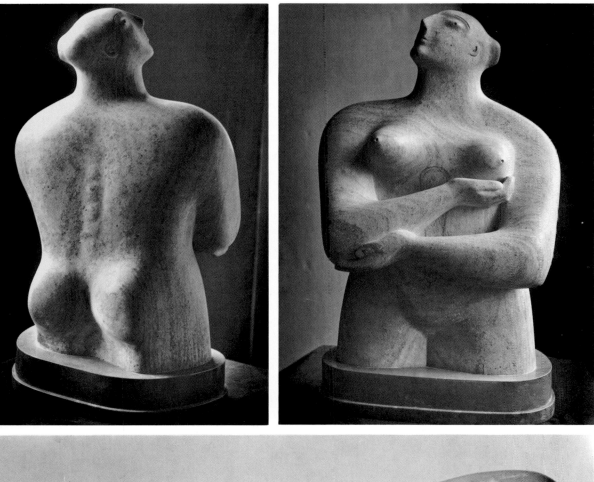

The liking for holes came about from wanting
to make space and three-dimensional form.
For me the hole is not just a round hole. It is
the penetration through from the front of the
block to the back. This was for me a revelation,
a great mental effort. It was having the idea to
do it that was difficult, and not the physical
effort. A very skilled gravestone memorial
carver can carve a chain. I remember seeing a
gravestone for a sailor, which had an anchor
with a chain. The links were free, carved out of
a solid piece of marble. It was very cleverly
done but it had not required a sculptor to do it.

Jasmine Cottage at Barfreston, our first country cottage. We used to go there for weekends and summer holidays and right next door we had this beautiful example of Romanesque architecture. The sea, Shakespeare Cliff and the country in between made a big impact on me. A good half of my year's work was done in the country during these holidays. In London I was teaching two days a week and seeing a lot of our friends. Thus I would save up ideas for the holidays. I had this wonderful desire always to get back to Barfreston, and later to Kingston, particularly in the summer when I could work fourteen to sixteen hours a day. When I come to look at how much work was done at Kingston, I am amazed. They were very happy days.

At this time Bernard Meadows began to help me. He was twenty-one. We would get up at six o'clock, throw a bucket of water over each other, have breakfast, and then work from half-past seven until eleven in the morning. Irina would make sandwiches and the three of us would go in our little car to Shakespeare Cliff, Dover, bathe, have a picnic meal, collect some pebbles and be back home by one or so in the afternoon. We would work until it was dark, eight or nine p.m. After supper I would draw until eleven or twelve at night, and we would be up again at six next morning. This was a regular routine we kept up. For recreation we would go to the cinema in Canterbury or Dover. The summer time was marvellous for one could count on so many full hours' work every day.

It was round about then that I was very aware of pebbles
and flints and they influenced my sculptures considerably.
I began separating forms from each other in order to be able
to relate space and form together. But of course one never
progresses in an absolutely straight line of development. The
content, or the expression of my feelings about the subject of
my work, inevitably interferes with my experiments . . . I go
backwards and forwards, and eventually some things work out
and incorporate a whole new point of view that I have been
trying to reach. This happens suddenly. This is the way that
life behaves.

Nobody is sure how flintstones came about. I think some were
formed by a natural casting process, since their strange shapes
could not possibly be caused by wind erosion or constant
wearing and fretting by the sea. The shapes of flintstones vary
in character in different parts of the country. Having
collected them for over fifty years on the beaches at
Broadstairs and in Norfolk and Dorset, I find a tremendous
difference in the type of flintstone in the various localities.

Flintstones, pebbles, shells and driftwood have all helped me
to start off ideas, but far more important to me has been the
human figure and its inner skeleton structure. You can feel
that a bone has had some sort of use in its life; it has
experienced tensions, has supported weights and has actually
performed an organic function, which a pebble has not done
at all. In themselves pebbles are dead forms, their shape is
accidental, and merely to copy them would not in itself create
a sculptural form. It is what I see in them that gives them
their significance.

These works are from 1933–4. Some of them are the relation of two forms to each other and the making of spaces between them and of the hole through the middle. Some are the realisation of the struggles I had had a year or two previously.

1
2

3
4

This work is in the Museum of Modern Art. Perhaps it can be thought of as a Mother and Child. I just called it "Two Forms". The bigger form has a kind of pelvic shape in it and the smaller form is like the big head of a child.

Although this sculpture looks abstract, it has organic elements. These are two separate forms—a head and a torso—but related with their base.

I used to carve from rock-chalk pebbles on the beach and then take home a full haversack to work on in the evenings. But unfortunately several of the little carvings that I did at the time later disintegrated.

5
6
7

8
9

Four individual variations—inventions of form, set side by side to make both a contrast and yet a unity of form.

A head and a smaller form—really two heads, a small head and a big head—but they are connected by space (that is the distance that they are apart).

I was using space in this four-piece reclining figure, in which there is the head part, the leg part, the body, and the small round form, which is the umbilicus and which makes a connection.

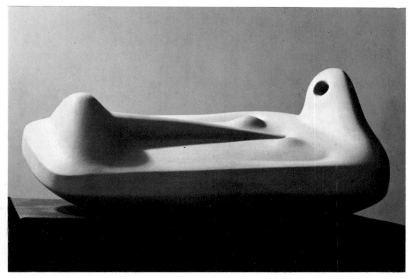

A wood sculpture that I think is 1935. It is really a family group. The relationship in the top part of the work is that between the head of the man, the woman's head, and the small head of the child—all growing out of a single base.

1

2
3

This was actually an ironstone pebble found on the beach in Norfolk. It was roughly this shape, but without the hole in it. To me it has an animal connection; it has got an expression of life. I was making something alive out of it.

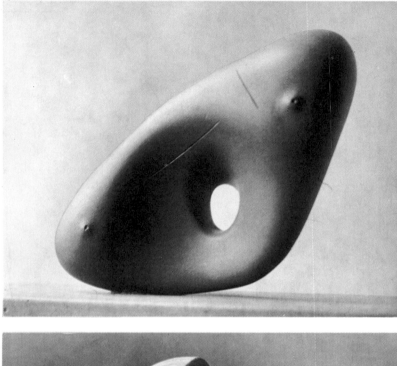

6

4
5

SUNDAY CINEMA BILL

Text of Measure Published

LOCAL OPTION PROPOSED

An End of the Common Informer

By Our Political Correspondent

Mr. Clynes' Sunday Performances (Regulation) Bill, which he introduced on April 2—the day the Commons adjourned for Easter—was issued yesterday.

As was anticipated, it gives power to County and County Borough Councils to grant licences; but only for musical and cinematograph entertainments, exhibitions of animals or inanimate objects, and debates.

Theatres are not included, but it is hardly likely that some members will not frame an amendment to bring them within the scope of the Bill should it get a second reading. That stage may possibly be taken some day in the week after next, and members will be free to vote as they like.

When any of the entertainments referred to in the Bill have been licensed the promoters will be freed from prosecution under the Sunday Observance Acts. Before, however, any local authority may grant a licence the Council must pass a resolution in favour of this step.

Moreover, the Council must be satisfied that the granting of such licences is "in accordance with a substantial demand in the locality"; the fact that a meeting is to be held to consider such a resolution must be advertised in the local Press at least fourteen days beforehand; and the authority "shall have regard to any representations made to them within such time and in such manner as may be specified in the notice."

THE PROFITS

There are other conditions, too, which are to be observed. The profits of any exhibition are to be ascertained by the licensing Council in accordance with regulations made by a Secretary of State and laid before Parliament. These profits are to go to "such charitable objects as may be approved" by the Council granting the licence.

Nor may a licence be granted unless it is arranged that no person is employed on Sunday who "has been employed in simi-

MODERN SCHOOL OF SCULPTURE

CULT OF UGLINESS TRIUMPHANT

MR. HENRY MOORE'S WORK

WANING INFLUENCE OF THE ELGIN MARBLES

By Our Art Critic

Those in favour of returning the Elgin Marbles to Greece could not find a better argument for their exodus than the sculpture at the Leicester Galleries, Leicester-square, by Mr. Henry Moore, who is one of the Professors at the Royal College of Art.

Mr. Courtenay Pollock and those who think with him could postulate that if works such as those at the Leicester Galleries can be produced by one who is responsible for the training of teachers in the chief national art school in England, then the Elgin Marbles have lost all their meaning as fragments of the greatest achievements in plastic art.

The cult of ugliness triumphs at the hands of Mr. Moore. He shows an utter contempt for the natural beauty of women and children, and in doing so, deprives even stone of its value as a means of æsthetic and emotional expression.

Examples such as the "Suckling Child" (1), the "Reclining Woman" (15), and Nos. 17, 23, and 29 make one doubt his seriousness. At anyrate, the figures referred to represent in this age of abundant disorder and intellectual self-starvation, the renunciation of the ideas, the forms, and the "austere logic of ancient sculpture" on which the permanent shape and spiritual significance of art are based.

MR. EPSTEIN'S COMMENT

There is no need to go back to negroid art for inspiration. There is still nobility of mind and grace of body to quicken the receptive and creative powers of men in art and literature. Æsthetic detachment is bound to atrophy soul and vision and lead to revolting formlessness such as offends sensitive people.

In fairness to Mr. Moore, read what Mr. Epstein writes in the catalogue introduction.

"Before these works," he writes, "I ponder in silence." Their "vast disproportions throw the shadow of our fears upon the background of space," and he feels "secret forces ready to burst forth on earth . . . to startle the unthinking out of their complacency. For the future of sculpture in England Henry Moore is vitally important."

EPSTEIN'S GENESIS

DISPUTE OVER EXHIBITION IN MANCHESTER

(FROM OUR OWN CORRESPONDENT)
MANCHESTER, Friday.

A SUNNY WEEK-END

WARM WEATHER TO CONTINUE

SPECIAL FORECASTS

The "Morning Post" publishes today a special forecast of the weather at the principal English holiday resorts for the week-end.

Conditions in London and the Southern half of England are expected to be mainly fair and rather warm. In the North and North-West the weather will be somewhat unsettled and mild. The special forecast is as follows:

BATH—*Cloudy; occasional showers.*
BOGNOR REGIS—*Fair periods.*
BOURNEMOUTH—*Fair periods.*
BRIGHTON—*Fair periods.*
CHELTENHAM—*Cloudy; occasional showers.*
CROMER—*Mainly fair.*
DEAL.—*Mainly fair.*
DOVER—*Mainly fair.*
EASTBOURNE—*Fair periods.*
FELIXSTOWE—*Mainly fair.*
FOLKESTONE—*Mainly fair.*
HASTINGS—*Fair periods.*
HARROGATE—*Cloudy; occasional rain.*
MARGATE—*Mainly fair.*
RYDE AND COWES—*Fair periods.*
SCARBOROUGH—*Fair intervals; showers.*
SHANKLIN AND VENTNOR—*Fair periods.*
SOUTHEND—*Mainly fair.*
SWANAGE—*Fair intervals.*
TORQUAY—*Fair intervals; showers.*
WINDERMERE—*Dull and showery.*

LONDON'S LEAD

Temperatures yesterday were more representative of May than of the beginning of April (writes our Meteorological Correspondent), and with a high pressure area over the Southern counties, genial sunshine of more than normal duration was widely experienced.

London, the warmest place in the country, reached 63 degrees, and enjoyed after a cloudy early morning, 7.4 hours of sunshine, while in the Western areas sunshine was even more generous.

Cloudier conditions obtained further to the north-west, where the Icelandic depression began to make its presence felt, but although this disturbance will gradually extend eastwards, fair and rather warm weather is likely to last over the Southern half of England throughout the week-end.

MAN TAKEN TO THREE HOSPITALS

SUFFERING FROM FRACTURED SKULL

The transference to three different hospitals of a man with a fractured skull received in a collision between a motor cycle, on which he was riding pillion, and a motor-van at Bedfont, was the subject of complaint by Thomas McCarthy, a valet of Brixton, at an inquest at Isleworth

This cutting refers to my first exhibition at the Leicester Galleries as a young sculptor. Epstein wrote a very nice foreword to the catalogue for me. Some of the criticisms in the Press upset me because I was teaching at the Royal College at the time and, since the Professor did not like my ideas or agree on my teaching, he used them against me. He showed them to Rothenstein, the Head of the Royal College, as a reason for having me removed and for allowing him to replace me with an assistant of his own choice. I'm told Rothenstein replied, "I believe in Moore. I appointed Moore for a seven year period and, as this period has not yet come to an end, he stays."

Epstein was remarkably generous and helpful to me as a young man from this time on. By 1931 he had already bought one or two sculptures of mine and he went on buying sculptures and drawings until 1937.

I do not think he began to sell any of them until after the war. It is quite natural for an older sculptor to be a little hurt or resentful, when in his opinion, a young sculptor commands too much attention. But we always remained friends right to the very end. Whenever we met it was always very pleasant. I respected and admired him enormously because he had borne the brunt of the Philistine attitude to sculpture. He had taken the whole cost on his shoulders from 1910 to 1940, and therefore I, for one, shall always be grateful to him. In those days sculpture seemed to anger the ordinary Philistine more than painting. I suppose this was because sculpture was so often outside on public view

Whilst touching some sculptures can give pleasure, touch itself is certainly not a criterion of good sculpture. A particular pebble or a marble egg may be delightful to feel or hold because it is very simple in shape and very smooth, whereas if it were the same shape but with a prickly or cold surface, you would not like touching it. Of course you can tell the shape of something if you can put your hands all round it. But it is impossible for a blind person to tell you the shape of a building. The same applies to a large sculpture, in that, although the sense of touch is fundamentally important and implied, it is not physically necessary to touch a sculpture in order to understand its form.

Also, I think a simple symmetrical shape eventually loses its interest because it is understood too quickly. A sculpture should have things about it you can go on discovering.

1/2/3

4/5

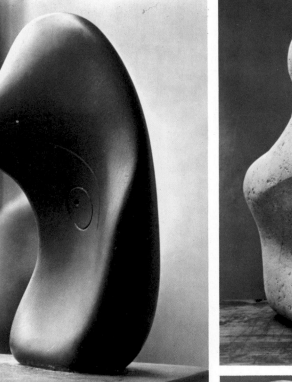

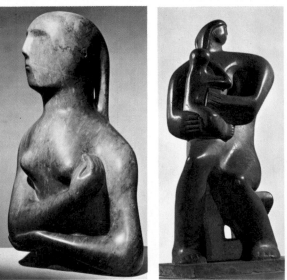

6/7/8

Most of the sculptures here are stone carvings. Stone for me has a blunt squareness, a squareness where you round off the corners. This seems a natural form for stone, and in fact I have called some of my sculptures "Square Form". On other occasions I have deliberately worked against the square idea, trying to eliminate the squareness of the original block. Thus, whilst most of the sculptures here are an obvious attempt to make squareness, a few others are fighting against it—opposites can imply each other.

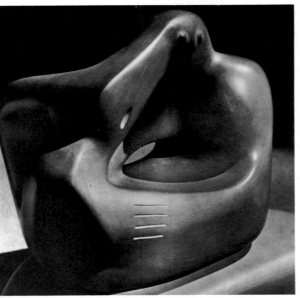

15

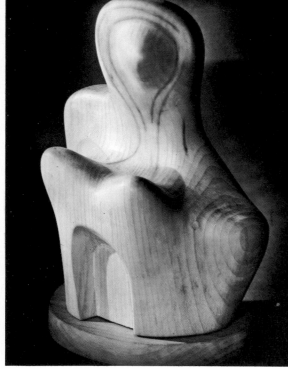

16

Three are in wood. The three-quarter length figure of a girl with clasped hands is in boxwood. It was carved out of a log about four inches in diameter and twelve inches long. Because I liked this piece of material and didn't want to waste any of it, I kept the head nearly as wide as the body.

17

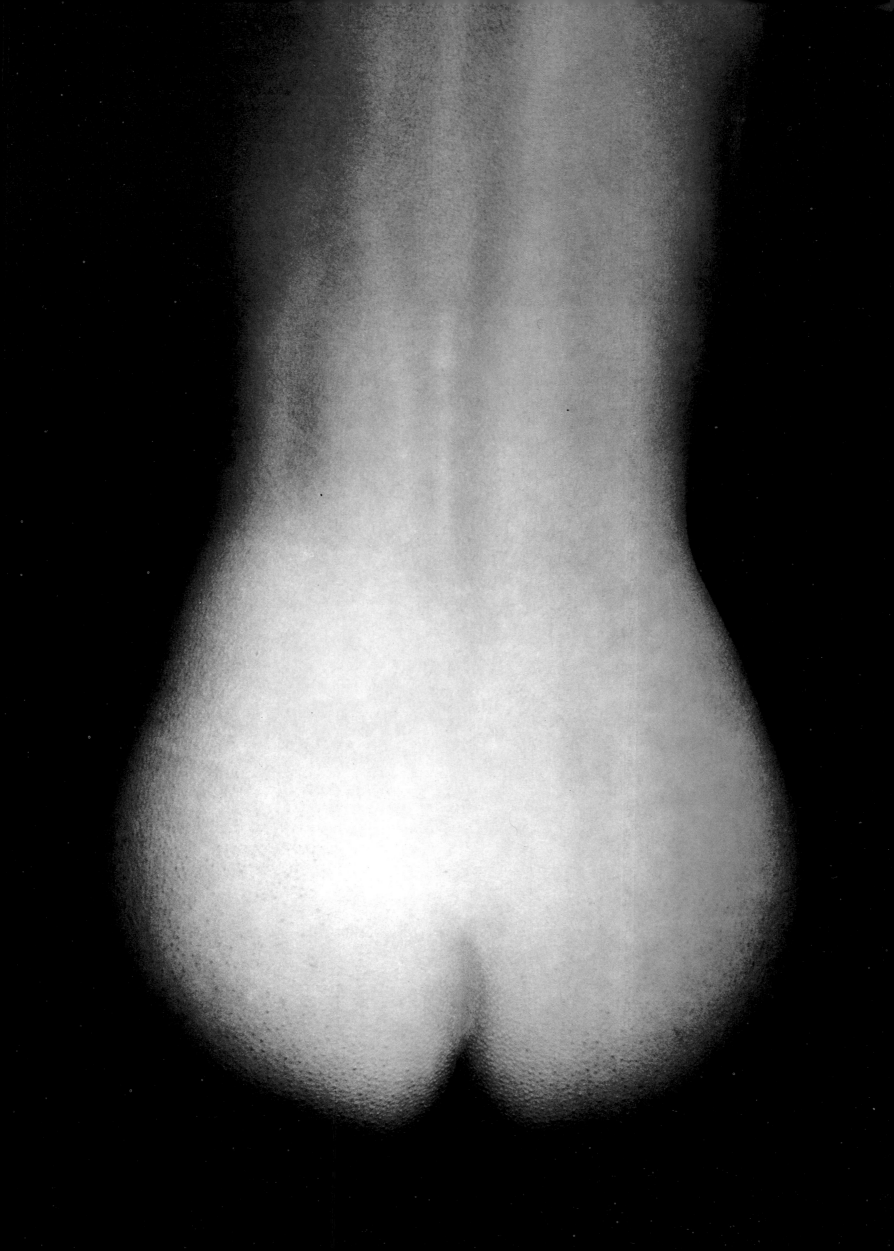

In 1934 we moved to Burcroft at
Kingston near Canterbury. The
cottage had five acres of wild meadow.
Here for the first time I worked with
a three or four mile view of the
countryside to which I could relate
my sculptures. The space, the
distance and the landscape became
very important to me as a background
and as an environment for my
sculpture. I particularly remember a
windmill on the skyline.

Shapes that stand out against the sky
are something I have always liked.

Out of doors in England the light is
as good for sculpture as anybody
could want. You have to make strong
forms that really exist because they
are not for ever flattered or
exaggerated by sunlight.

A wood carver lived opposite our
house at Kingston. He did mainly
church work. He was a very nice old
boy, but very puzzled with the
things I was doing.

I went to the stone quarries in Derbyshire and bought a lot of random blocks of Hopton Wood stone. I had room and space enough at Burcroft to let the stones stand around in the landscape, and seeing them daily gave me fresh ideas for sculpture. Some of the stones were six or seven feet long and very odd shapes. The sculptures on these, and the next four pages, are some of those I made at the time. This was very much a stone period in my life. In fact up to the war, nine out of ten sculptures I did were in stone. I still love stone.

1/2/3

1

2

3

I always have a vague idea of what I want to do, which only emerges when the time comes to do it. Sculpture is different from drawing and painting in that you have to sustain your ideas so much longer. Otherwise you would be starting a new sculpture every day and you would never finish any of them. Carving is a relatively slow craft, so the smallest carving takes a week. When my sculpture was mainly carving I would be having many more ideas than I was able to carry out and I would get rid of ideas, if that is the right phrase, by drawing to prevent them from blocking each other up. Often I would make pages of drawings of ideas. On one sheet of paper there could be as many as thirty projects, such as Stringed Figures, all produced in a few hours. One of them would hold my attention and I would think it was the best one. And then I would have to settle down to the longer job of making it into a sculpture. People often ask me how I have the patience to do stone carving. My answer is that I have adjusted myself to my craft.

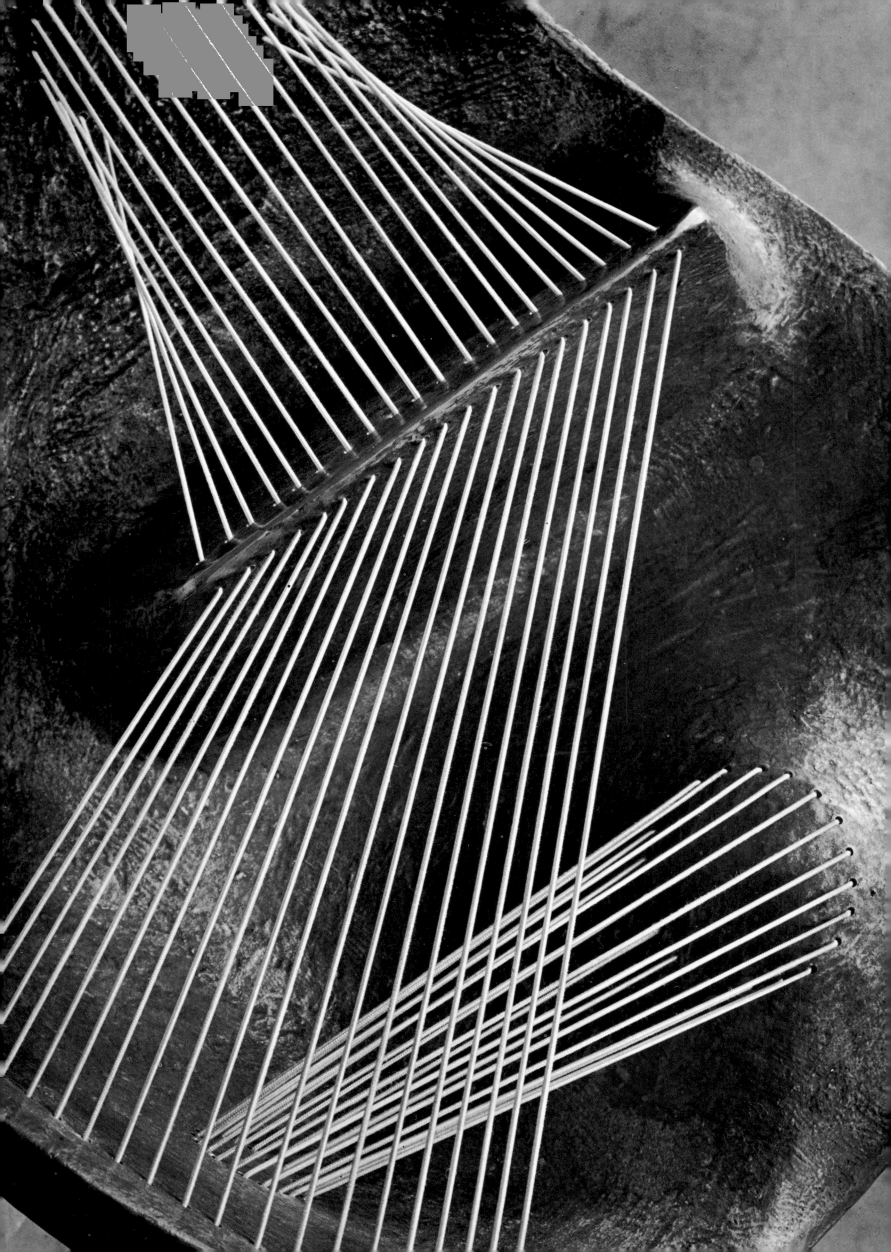

Undoubtedly the source of my stringed figures was the Science Museum. Whilst a student at the R.C.A. I became involved in machine art, which in those days had its place in modern art. Although I was interested in the work of Léger, and the Futurists, who exploited mechanical forms, I was never directly influenced by machinery as such. Its interest for me lies in its capacity for movement, which, after all, is its function.

I was fascinated by the mathematical models I saw there, which had been made to illustrate the difference of the form that is halfway between a square and a circle. One model had a square at one end with twenty holes along each side, making eighty holes in all. Through these holes strings were threaded and led to a circle with the same number of holes at the other end. A plane interposed through the middle shows the form that is halfway between a square and a circle. One end could also be twisted to produce forms that would be terribly difficult to draw on a flat surface. It wasn't the scientific study of these models but the ability to look through the strings as with a bird cage and to see one form within another which excited me.

I didn't as a student use this idea and it was nearly fourteen years later that it became a definite influence in my sculpture. Even then I did stringed figures only for two or three years, as I found, after a period, that the use of strings in sculpture was almost too ingenious, too easy.

In one afternoon I could draw fifty or sixty ideas, all of which would, if I had carried them out, have been interesting and intricate, so much so that it was more a matter of invention than imagination.

I don't give my sculptures high-falutin' or abstruse Greek titles. I prefer to call them "Reclining Figure" or "Mother and Child", simple descriptive names.

I decide the title of a sculpture after I have finished it. I didn't set out to do a sculpture called "The Bird Basket" or "The Bride" or even one called "The King and Queen". The naming of a piece of sculpture can start a line of thought for the person looking at it. I'm sure Paul Klee gave most of his paintings and drawings their titles after they were finished— or while working on them. There's one of Klee's pictures with lines going into water and forms underneath. He called it "They're Biting" as though it showed a fisherman on the river bank dropping his line into the water and then getting excited that the fish were biting. A fuller appreciation eventually comes because it makes the observer look for the title's connection.

Take the sculpture "The Bird Basket". It has got an organic form to it although the strings are abstract straight lines. The carving is in lignum vitae wood and at one end is the head and the other end the tail. When I was working on it. I used to pick it up like a basket by the loop over the top. So the two words "Bird" and "Basket" are significant because they were arrived at in a practical way.

1

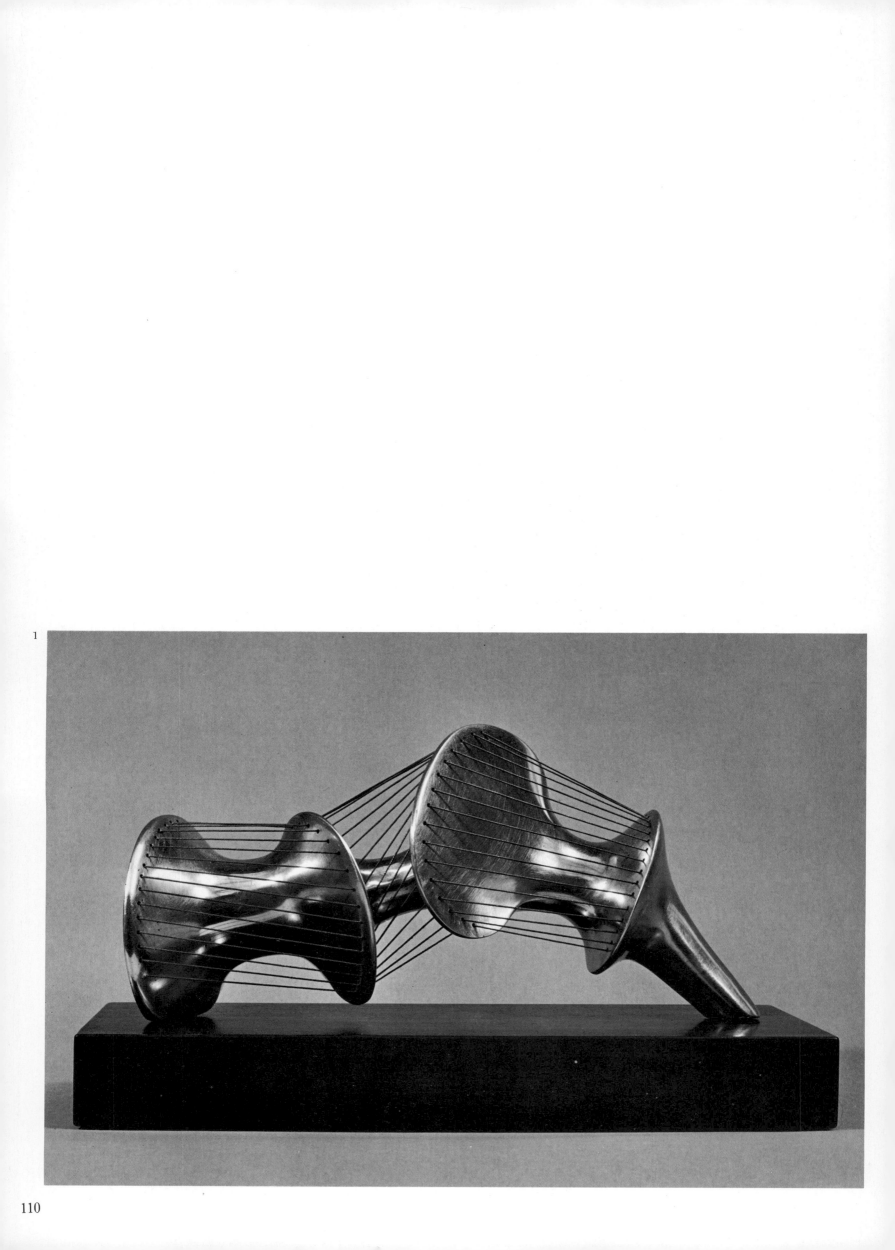

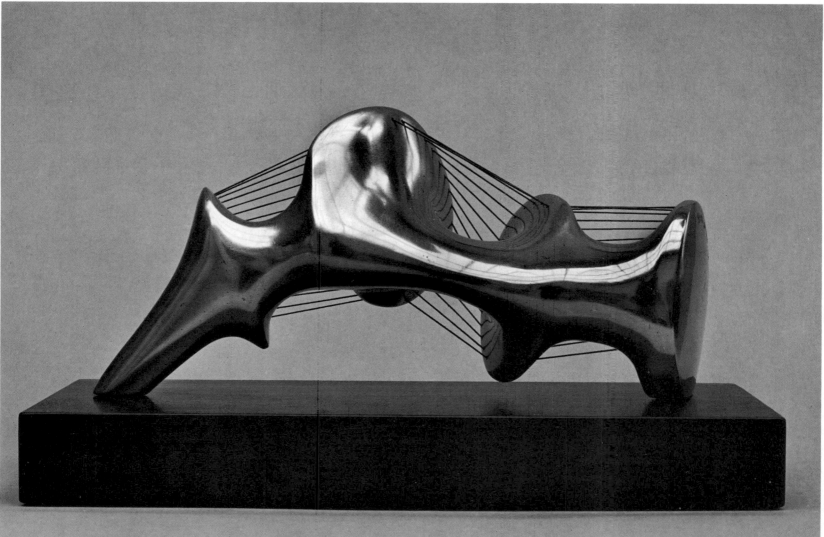

1/2

3

4

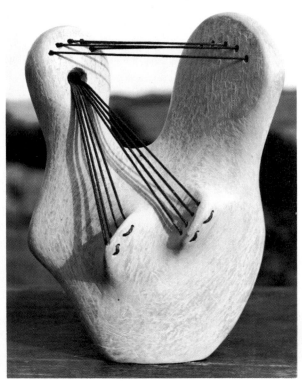

5/6

7

The asymmetrical growth of trees responding to their environment has always interested me. If a branch starts to go one way and there isn't enough sunlight or space that way, it will change direction and find its own area to live in.

A Bond Street Studio
Portrait

Sailing on Norfolk Broads.
1930

HM with Reclining elm-wood
Figure, just finished at
Burcroft. 1939.

Me + Irina, the McWilliams,
the Gerrards + relations
in Derbyshire

After a bathe
at Shakespeare
Cliff - Dover.

Graham Sutherland
H.M
and Myfanwy Piper
picnicing in train
on way to Northampton, for
unveiling of Madonna + Child

Choosing stone
at Hopton Wood
Quarry in Derbyshire

116

Me &
1929 — Irina ~~XXX~~, on holiday
with the Coxons & the
Hughes-Stantons — in Suffolk.

Passport Photograph.

Tennis, my favorite game

Irina, pensive
photographed
by me.

⟹ Me + Irina
Taken by a Japanese photographer.

Irina & HM, having tea in
Garden at Hoglands, during
the war.   Me in Home Guard
Sitting Gaily, on   uniform
a dry stone wall
in Yorkshire.
Photo taken by Ruth Gill
a student of mine at Chelsea School of Art.

117

Eventually I found that form and space are one and the same thing. You can't understand space without understanding form.

For example, in order to understand form in its complete three-dimensional reality you must understand the space that it would displace if it were taken away. You can't measure a space without measuring from one point to another. The heavens have space that we can understand because there are points—the stars and the sun—that are different distances away from each other. In the same way we can only see space in a landscape by relating the foreground and middle distance to the far distance. To understand the distance from my thumb to my forefinger needs exactly the same understanding as distances in landscape.

The trouble is that when so many young sculptors think they are now dealing with space, which sculptors of the past such as Michelangelo never did, they just don't understand three-dimensional form. You can use a method, or a technique, which gives you space without having to think about it. You can use objects that are pieced together and construct them so that they stick out into space, and therefore you can't help but get space. This is nothing to do with the emotional comprehension of space and, even though it may be claimed as "spatial" sculpture, it may only be that the method has produced it, not the artist. Rembrandt's late paintings and drawings show that his understanding of reality, of three-dimensional form and space, was infinitely greater than our so-called "space" sculptors.

In my opinion there is both a "surrealist" element and an "abstract" element in all good art. There is the mixture of emotional or imaginative non-logical inspiration, which is the surrealist point of view, combined with the artist's experience and idealism about the art that he practises. The abstract element includes a sense of design so that there is some composition or unity as well as imaginative content. I would not myself want to be called either a purely abstract artist or purely surrealist—a "pop" or an "op" artist, or given any label like that. No one can escape being influenced by both past and present art. The artist is a product of his time. Someone like Cézanne shows in his early periods the influences of innumerable artists, such as Courbet, Delacroix, El Greco, Pisarro, Daumier and many others. It proves that he contemplated and appreciated qualities in other artists and their work. But in the end he came through with a personal contribution that is unlike any of the others. The same applies to Turner who, up to fifty, was imitating Claude and other artists he admired—and yet he ended by producing astonishingly original and revolutionary work.

You don't set out to go in any one direction. Instead you respond to whatever influences come into your experience. I would say that primitive art has been a most important influence with me. But when I began as a young (art) student, only Renaissance and Greek art were appreciated. And it was outside art school, by reading Roger Fry's *Vision and Design* in Leeds Reference Library that I began to appreciate Negro sculpture and other primitive art. However, the greatest influence in my sculpture is the study of the human figure. My work is a mixture of influences and appreciation of art and my excitement and observation of nature. I think this is what all art has been. You can't point to any one artist who is purely a product of himself alone. Perhaps the largest influence in Michelangelo's life was the discovery of the Belvedere Torso which came to light early in his career and from then onwards coloured his whole attitude to sculpture.

To me, Michelangelo's achievement has always seemed superhuman. It is like a poet realising the unbelievable achievement of Shakespeare's poetry.

I should say that in my personal outlook, the greatest influence has probably been novels. As a young man, the Russian novelists Dostoyevsky and Tolstoy, and then later Stendhal, Thomas Hardy and D. H. Lawrence had an enormous influence on my point of view in life and therefore on my sculpture too. Roger Fry's book opened my eyes and introduced me to ideas that were already current in France. He pointed out things which I could then follow up.

I think about sculpture all the time. I have seen a great deal of the sculpture of the past. I work at it in my studio for ten to twelve hours a day. I even dream about it. If as a result I was only to produce something that everyone immediately understood, I would not have been thinking very profoundly. Surely you would expect a special tuning of my mind, something new, something different.

I try to be direct and practical in all my work. A sculptor has to be because so much of his work is essentially practical. It's no good him being just a theoretician. His ideas have to end up solid.

People should not be impressed by things they do not comprehend, and should certainly not permit themselves to be belittled by them. Obscurity for its own sake only impresses fools. At the same time, I do not mean that everything needs to be obvious.

Form—the shape of things—is the most exciting side of my life. Through it I express my visions and my reactions. In making sculpture, I do not think in words, I think in shapes. If something is wrong with a sculpture I know it and I try to make it right, not by logical argument but by a process of eliminating what is wrong.

Your past controls your future. You cannot escape it. I don't want to know how I work. I would hate to be psychoanalysed. If I am abnormal, that may be my contribution to Society. No artist should try to understand himself too much. So much in nature is an accident. In the same way art is unplanned. Today, for instance, I did not go to the studio, but if I had done I might have created something better than anything I have done in the last ten years. I don't know if I will go tomorrow. Art tends to arrive at a true result through instinct.

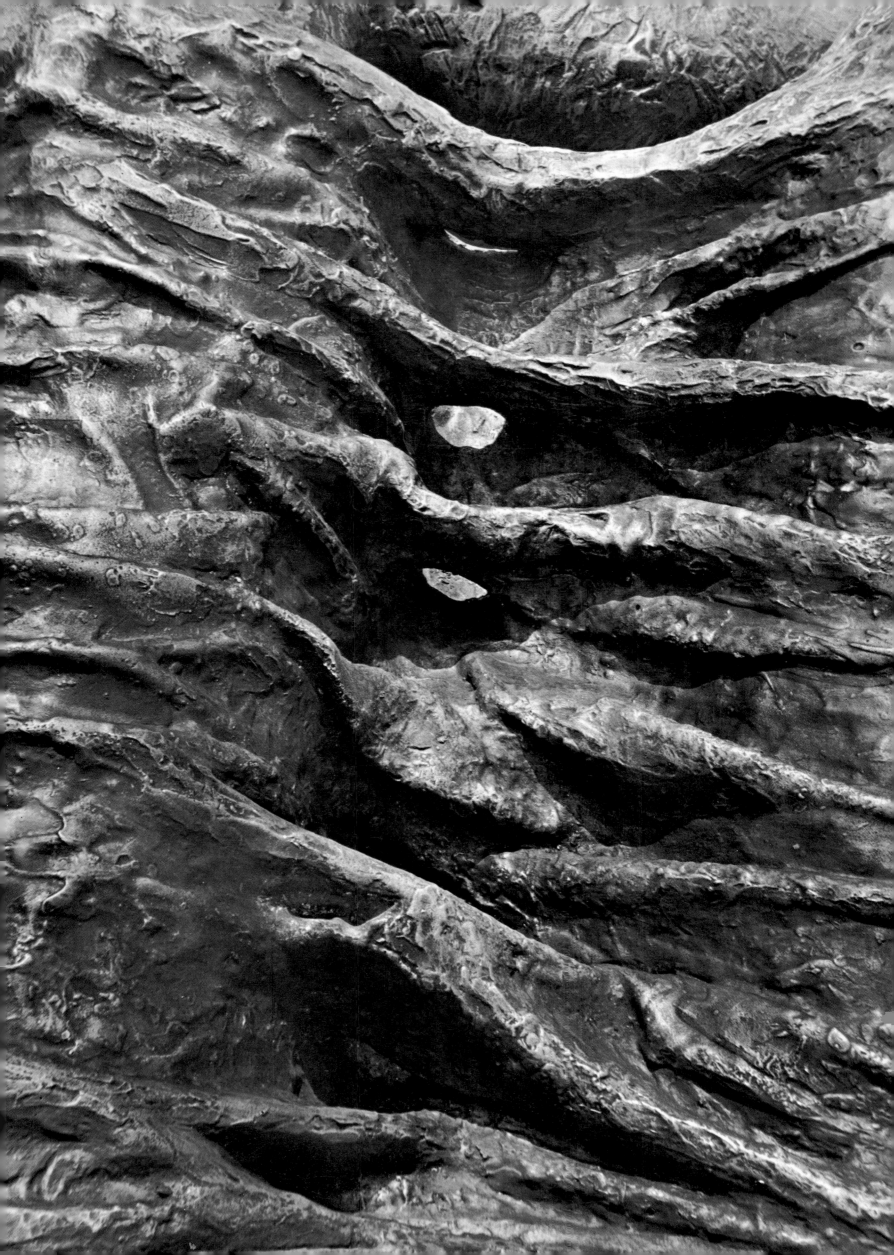

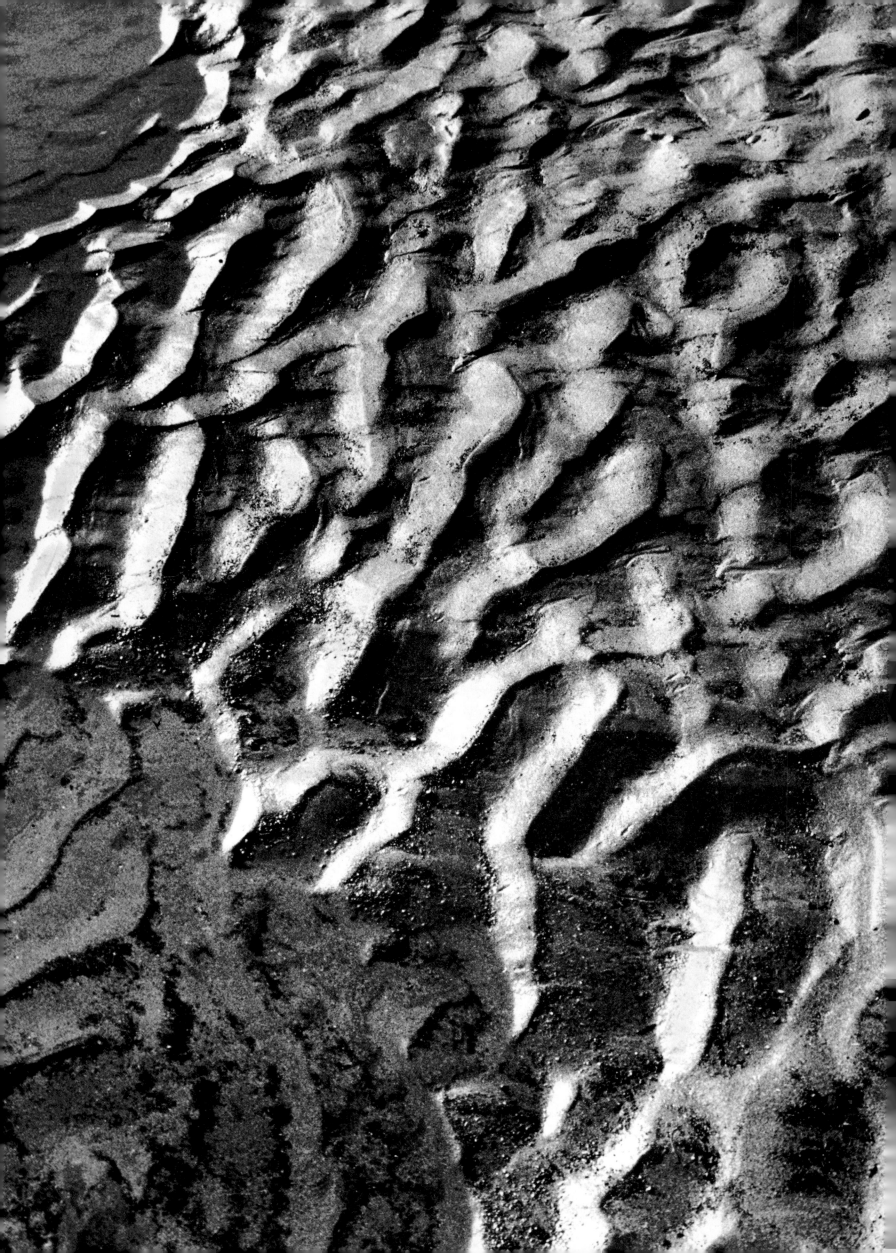

Besides the human form, I am tremendously excited by all natural forms, such as cloud formations, birds, trees and their roots, and mountains, which are to me the wrinkling of the earth's surface, like drapery. It is extraordinary how closely ripples in the sand on the seashore resemble the gouge marks in wood carving.

The upright exterior-interior form, opposite, is like the petals which enclose the stamen of a flower. Besides acting as a protection, they provide an attraction.

After war was declared I continued for a time to live at Burcroft, although it was made a restricted area. I was very fond of the cottage and was working well there.

Chelsea School of Art, where I was teaching two days a week, was attached to the Chelsea Polytechnic and we were informed that the Poly was instituting a course in precision tool-making. Graham Sutherland and I volunteered for this course and we were told to be prepared to start at any moment.

As a result Irina and I left Burcroft and went to live at my studio at 11a Parkhill Road. Shortly afterwards we accepted the offer of No. 7, Mall Studios from Ben Nicholson and Barbara Hepworth, who had decided to evacuate to Cornwall because of their children.

Every day I expected to hear from Chelsea Polytechnic that the course was about to begin. Consequently there seemed to be no point in starting work on a new sculpture and so I concentrated on drawings. Then came the Battle of Britain, and I was still waiting to hear from the Polytechnic when the blitz began.

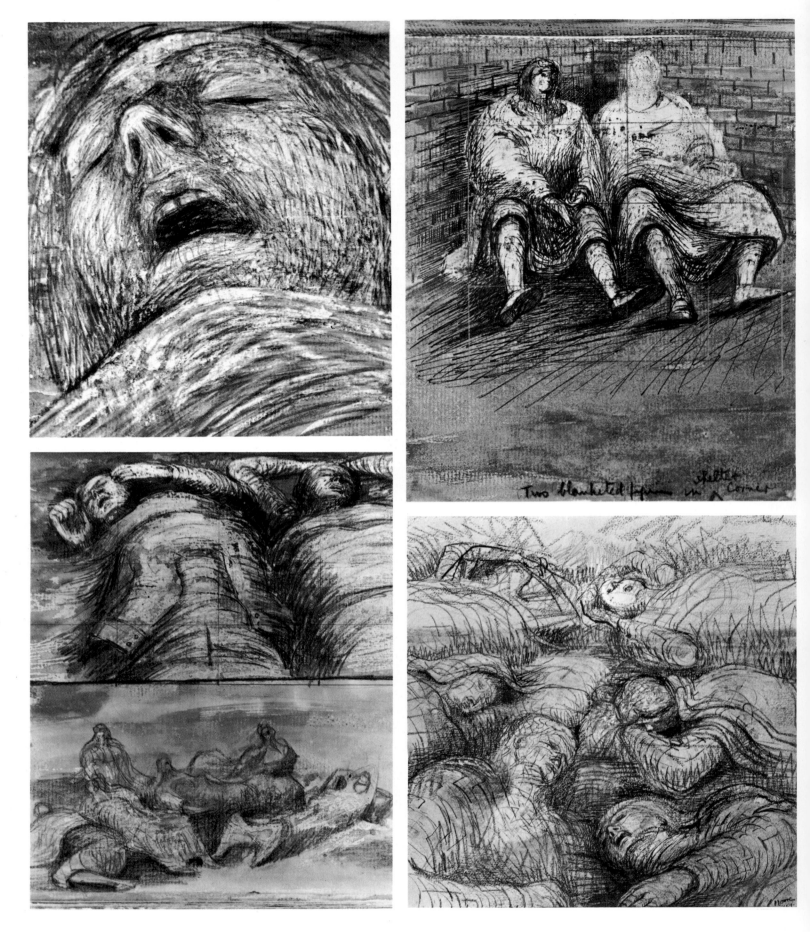

Two blanketed figures in shelter corner

One evening after dinner in a restaurant with some friends we returned home by Underground taking the Northern Line to Belsize Park. As a rule I went into town by car and I hadn't been by Tube for ages. For the first time that evening I saw people lying on the platforms at all the stations we stopped at. When we got to Belsize Park we weren't allowed out of the station for an hour because of the bombing. I spent the time looking at the rows of people sleeping on the platforms. I had never seen so many reclining figures and even the train tunnels seemed to be like the holes in my sculpture. And amid the grim tension, I noticed groups of strangers formed together in intimate groups and children asleep within feet of the passing trains.

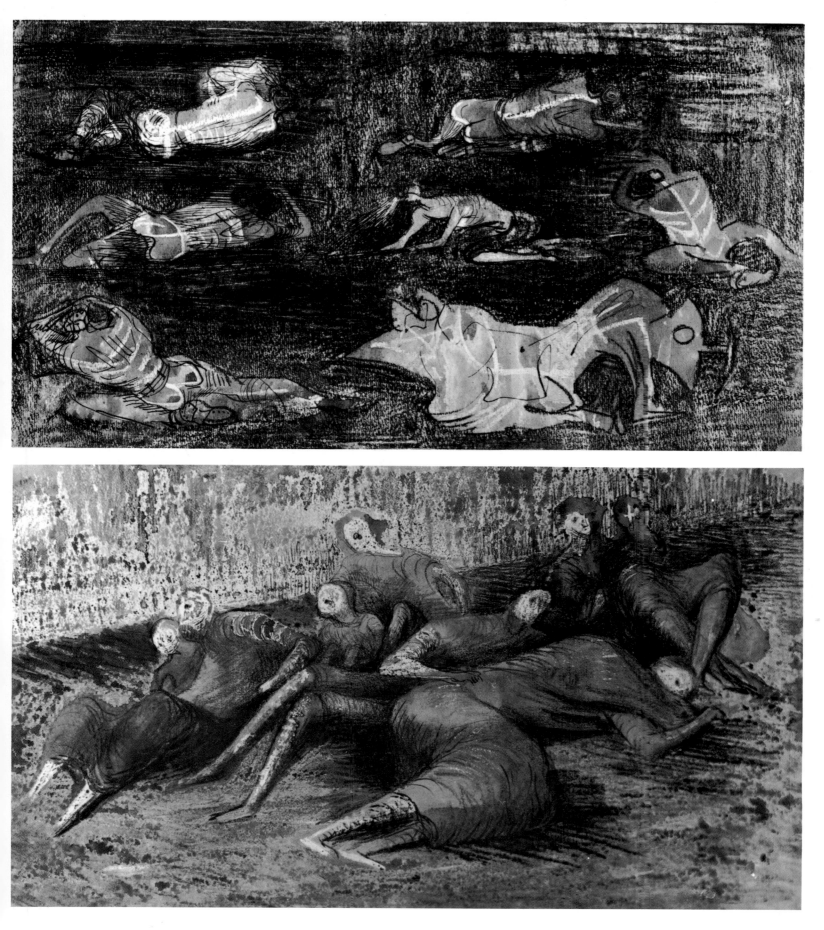

After that evening I travelled all over London by
Underground. I was already drawing and I now wanted to
draw what I saw in the shelters.
I never made any sketches in the Underground. It would have
been like drawing in the hold of a slave ship. I would wander
about sometimes passing a particular group that interested
me half a dozen times. Sometimes, in a corner where I could
not be seen, I would make notes on the back of an envelope
so that I would be reminded when I sketched next day.

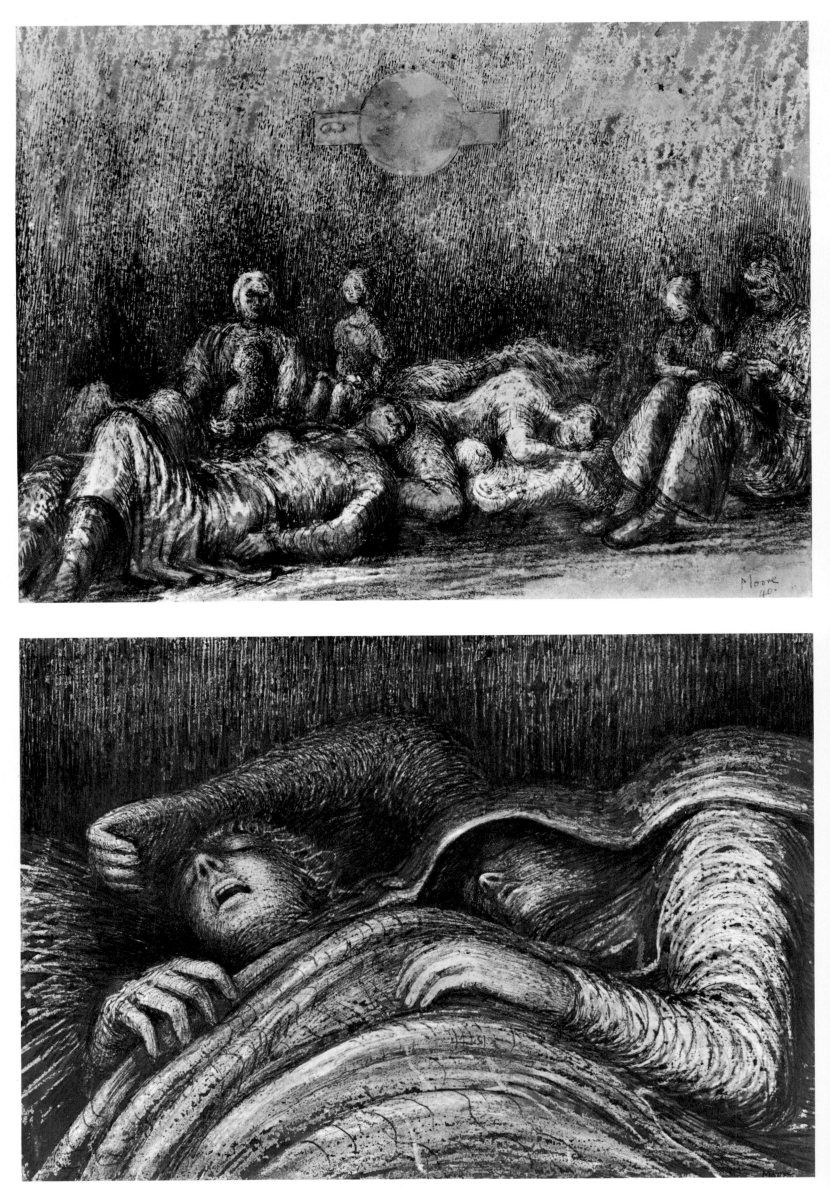

One day Kenneth Clark saw some of these sketches and told me that I could no longer refuse to become an official war artist. He was Chairman of the War Artists Committee and when he had asked me at the beginning of the war, I had declined.

I started a sketch book full of ideas for drawings to be carried out later and notes that I had made in the Tube. The first sketch book now belongs to Kenneth Clark. As soon as I had finished it, I started another which I gave to Irina. Although I started two others, neither of them have survived.

One weekend the Labour M.P. Leonard Matters, who was a friend of ours, invited us to stay with him at Much Hadham. Returning to London on Monday we found Parkhill Road roped off and a warden informed us that the Mall Studios had been flattened. Although in fact he was wrong, my studio had suffered badly from the blast and was a shambles of broken glass. Fortunately only one of the sculptures had been damaged. Since obviously we had to leave the studio I asked Leonard Matters if we could stay with him at Much Hadham until we could find somewhere else.

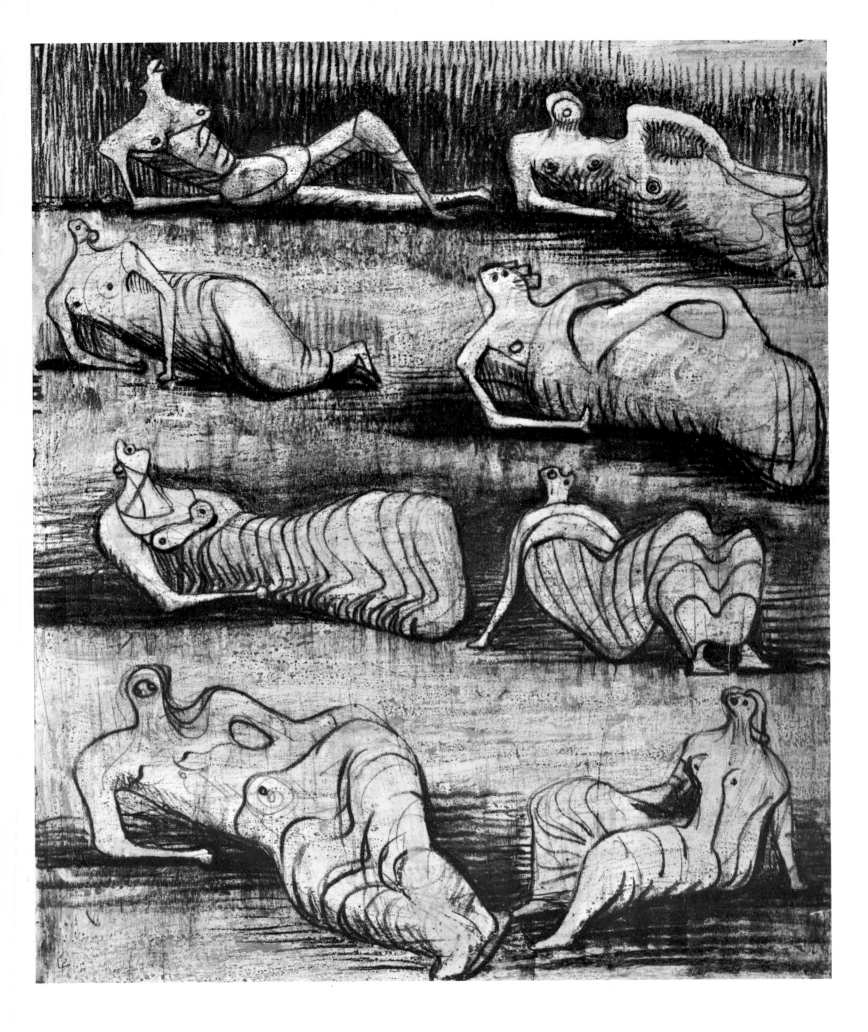

At Much Hadham, we discovered that we could lease half of a house called "Hoglands". The owner was away at the war and his wife and children were living in the other half. A month or so later the wife decided to go and live with her mother and offered to sell us Hoglands. I had just been offered £300 by Gordon Onslow-Ford for the big 1939 elmwood "Reclining Figure" and this happened to be exactly the deposit required on the house. We have lived at Hoglands ever since.

I used to go to London two days a week spending the nights in the Underground and coming up at dawn. Then I would return to Hoglands and spend two days sketching. The rest of the time I spent working on drawings to show the War Artists Committee. I would show them eight or ten at a time and they would choose four or five leaving me to do what I liked with the rest.

Naturally, of the Underground stations, I had my favourites. I used to go quite often to Cricklewood and I was fascinated by a huge shelter at Tilbury which was in fact the basement of a warehouse. But Liverpool Street Underground Extension was the place that interested me most. The new tunnel had been completed except for the rails and at night its entire length was·occupied by a double row of sleeping figures.

I sketched with pen and ink, wax crayons and watercolour, using the wax-resist technique which I had discovered by accident before the war. I had been doing a drawing for my three-year-old niece using two or three wax crayons. Wishing to add some more colour, I found a box of watercolour paints and was delighted to see the watercolour run off the parts of the drawing that had a surface of wax. It was like magic and I found it very useful when doing my sketch books.

Early in 1941 the authorities started to provide bunks and canteens in the shelters and to lay on sanitary arrangements. With them the drama and the strangeness of the early months in the Underground began to recede both for me and for the people themselves. Mentioning this to Herbert Read one day he suggested that, with my background, coal-mining, being an industry of great national importance, would make a good subject.

I spent two weeks in a coal-mine and, since the miners knew what I was there for, I was able to make my sketches on the spot. These sketches provided me with enough material for about three months of drawing.

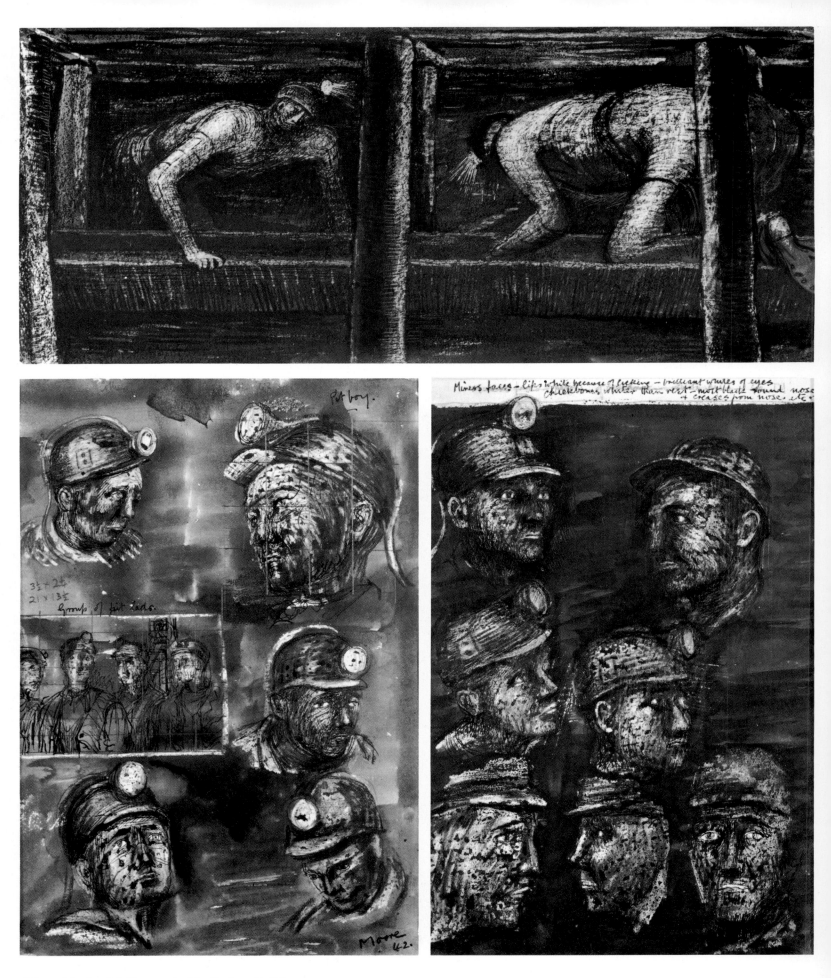

After this I told Kenneth Clark that I did not want to undertake any more commissions and I began to work once again on drawings for sculpture. Towards the end of 1942, I held an exhibition of fifty new drawings at Kurt Valentin's Gallery in New York, which did not include any shelter or coal-mine drawings.

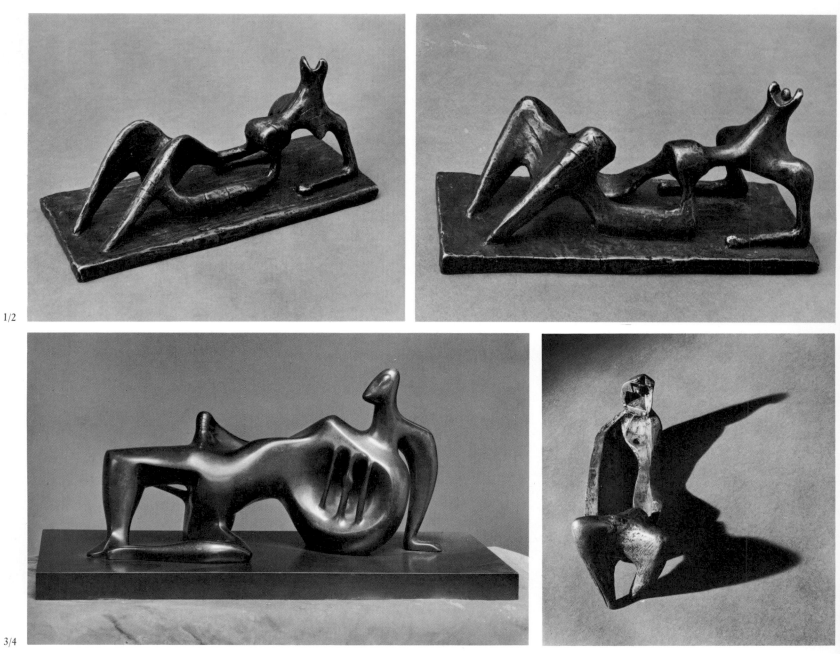

1/2

3/4

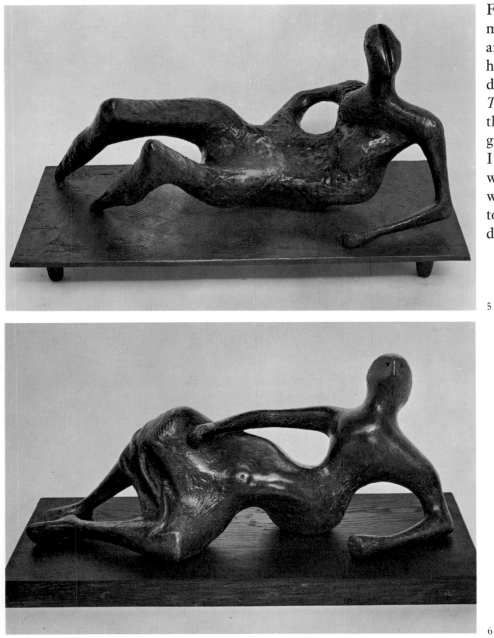

From the very beginning the reclining figure has been my main theme. The first one I made was around 1924, and probably more than half of my sculptures since then have been reclining figures. This obsession of mine is discussed and explained in great detail in a book called *The Archetypal World of Henry Moore* by Erich Neumann, the favourite disciple of Jung. I began reading it but gave up half-way through the first chapter as I decided I did not want to be psycho-analysed, nor understand what makes me tick—either I would like and agree with what he said and be tempted to work to a programme to prove him right, or I would disagree and try to disprove what I didn't like about his theory.

5

6

1

As a house is the home of a family, so is a city the home of its inhabitants, and should be furnished with works of art, just as you would furnish your own home. I think London could easily have three times as many monuments, sculptures and fountains than it has at present. It would make it a much happier place in which to live.

The Victorians to a certain extent added a romantic interest to their buildings, particularly their railway stations. Although their statues of aldermen and civic dignitaries are very dull and often very poor sculpture, they give some interest to our streets. Naturally I wish they could have made London something like Bernini's Rome.

A little step forward has been made recently with temporary open-air sculpture exhibitions such as at Battersea, although these exhibitions have now become overcrowded like museums, where you cannot concentrate on a single sculpture because your eyes are distracted by all the other sculptures in too close proximity.

It should be possible for sculptures to be rearranged in a city in the way you rearrange possessions in your home. If you do not like a piece somewhere, you try it elsewhere, and, in doing so, see it in a new way. It becomes part of your life, and in this way sculptures could become part of the life of a city.

Hoglands

"The Northampton Madonna and Child" was one of the most difficult and heart-searching sculptures that I ever tried to do. Possibly it is the only sculpture of mine that can be called a commission. For my other sculptures that have been used in public, such as the Unesco "Reclining Figure" or even the figure on the St James' Underground Station, which was the very first piece of public sculpture I did, I was using my own subject matter and sometimes I had already made the maquettes. As in the Lincoln Center figure I was doing what I would have done anyway, except, in this case, I made it larger to make the correct scale for the architecture and its surroundings.

I doubt if I would ever have attempted a religious subject had it not been for the continuous pressure and encouragement from Canon Hussey. The Mother and Child theme had been a common one to nearly half my work. Yet I hesitated over his request because I realised that I should not do an ordinary Mother and Child, put it in a church and call it a Madonna and Child. Anyway, I told Canon Hussey that I felt uncertain whether I could really produce a piece of sculpture that I would be sure in my own conscience, in my own heart, was suitable, and therefore I would first do some drawings and maquettes. After three months of making drawings and doing some eight or nine maquettes, I was still uncertain, and so I asked my friends Sir Kenneth Clark, Herbert Read and others whose opinions I respect, to have a look and to confirm whether I had achieved what was right for a church.

It was a real worry, and gave me many problems. There were all sorts of
implications other than purely sculptural ones. One problem lay in trying to make
the child an intellectual-looking child, that you could believe might have more of
a future than just an ordinary baby.
The face of the Madonna has got a certain aloof mystery.

The idea of the family group crystallised before the war. Henry Morris, the Director of Education for Cambridgeshire, asked me to do a sculpture for the Impington Village College, the first of the modern schools in England. It had been designed by Walter Gropius. As the College was going to be used for adult education as well, the idea of connecting parents and children came into my mind. I think that the first family group drawings and maquettes were done in 1935–6, although I didn't actually make the full-size sculpture until later.

There was a period when the Church was the greatest patron of the arts, but in the last two or three hundred years the Church has gradually abandoned the good artists in favour of those who have been taught to produce religious art for its own sake. One knows from the so-called religious art shops connected with the Roman Catholic Church and the Church of England that the standard is terribly poor— sentimental, sweet and sloppy. Religion no longer seems to provide inspiration or impetus for many artists. And yet all art is religious in a sense that no artist would work unless he believed that there was something in life worth glorifying. This is what art is about. There is of course a difference between a work of art which is contemplated for a church and one which is intended for a house, a museum or a street. It was this difference that caused me all the trouble and the doubts about doing the Northampton "Madonna and Child". The same doubts remain over my doing any work for the Church.

For example, I have been asked to do a Crucifixion, but this would make me have the same misgivings all over again. In my work each sculpture usually grows out of the last one, without any conscious programme. Thus the Glenkiln Cross is a crucifix, although I didn't deliberately set out to make it that. It was an upright motif idea which developed into a worn-down rudimentary cross.

If I agreed to do a subject from someone else's suggestion, it would mean stopping work on whatever else I was doing. This is the reason why I dislike and refuse commissions.

However, the Crucifixion is such a universal theme that I may attempt it one day. Everybody thinks more often of death as they grow older, unless they are too occupied or too extrovert. An artist can't be either. When you are young you don't think so realistically about death. Now I often think about it.

"Mother and Child" at Claydon Church, Suffolk.

1

2

3

4

The three Battersea "Standing Figures" in Darley Dale
sandstone, are probably the first big sculptures that showed
the influence of my war drawings. Although the figures are
static, I made them look into the distance, as if they were
expecting something dramatic to happen. Drama can be
implied without the appearance of physical action.

THREE STANDING FIGURES
HENRY MOORE

The Dartington Hall "Reclining Figure" was done as a memorial to Christopher Martin, an old friend of mine who had been art director at Dartington. I chose an idea which was calm and peaceful and seemed to me to be most suitable. But at the same time, in my studio I was doing a large wood sculpture which was very different in spirit. This was at a time when I was catching up on the two years of sculpture time I had lost through the war and I had many accumulated ideas to get rid of. And so I was doing two sculptures at the same time although the two were completely different from each other in mood.

Thus I was able to satisfy both sides of my nature by working on the rather gentle Dartington figure at the same time as the Cranbrook Reclining Figure in elmwood, which for me had great drama, with its big beating heart like a great pumping station.

The theory that the work of an artist or a novelist is directly attributable to his personality is a romantic one. An artist's gift is that he can project his imagination. Balzac, for example, carried away on his imagination could write continuously for days and nights on end, living in his mind the lives of his characters. It doesn't mean that if you write about sorrowful things you are in reality miserable. And yet, of course, an artist uses experiences he's had in life. Such an experience in my life was the birth of my daughter Mary, which re-invoked in my sculpture my Mother and Child theme. A new experience can bring to the surface something deep in one's mind.

Drawings of Mary after being bathed. They remind me very strongly of the tremendous excitement and pleasure her birth gave me. Very young babies have always fascinated me; the big head, the frog-like quality of the body, and their kicking vitality.

This plaster detail of the Tate "Family Group" shows the arms of the mother and the father with the child forming a knot between them, tying the three into a family unity.

9

177

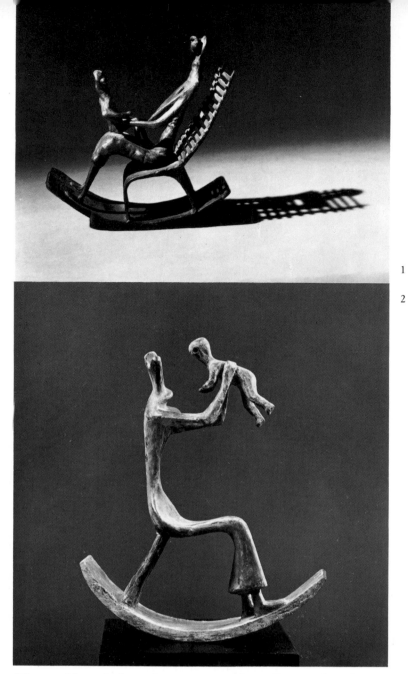

1
2
3

The rocking chair sculptures were done for my daughter Mary, as toys which actually rock. I discovered while doing them that the speed of the rocking depended on the curvature of the base and the disposition of the weights and balances of the sculpture, so each of them rocks at a different speed.

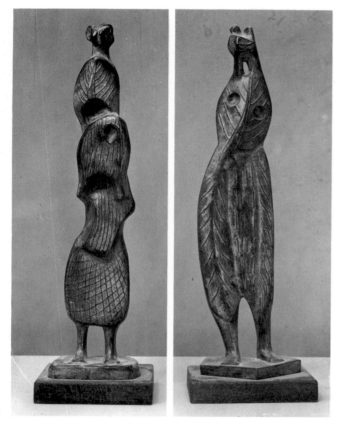

I only did two leaf-figure sculptures, but I did many leaf-figure drawings (from which I made etchings later). I don't know what led me to do them, but maybe I saw sculptural possibilities in the leaves I picked up and the plants I noticed in the garden as I walked from my house to the studio.

One day you see things which the day before you had never noticed. Life is like that, and certainly many of my ideas happen that way.

1

This sculpture "Helmet Head" is intended to be sinister, like a face peering out from inside a prison. There are two versions, one in bronze and one in lead. The lead version, I think, is more expressive because lead has a kind of poisonous quality; you feel that if you licked it you might die.

2

3

I cast these small sculptures myself in a little foundry I built at the bottom of the garden. In some of them, I liked the "runners" in relationship to the sculpture and so I left them on. In this way I took advantage of the technique of lost-wax bronze casting.

4

When you cast bronze, you cannot always just pour the molten bronze into the mould like pouring water into a jug, because air-pockets would become trapped within the intricate shapes in the mould, making the cast incomplete. Therefore wax "runners" are added to connect the sculpture throughout, so

5

The "Festival Reclining Figure" is perhaps my first sculpture where the space and the form are completely dependent on and inseparable from each other. I had reached the stage where I wanted my sculpture to be truly three-dimensional. In my earliest use of holes in sculpture, the holes were features in themselves. Now the space and the form are so naturally fused that they are one.

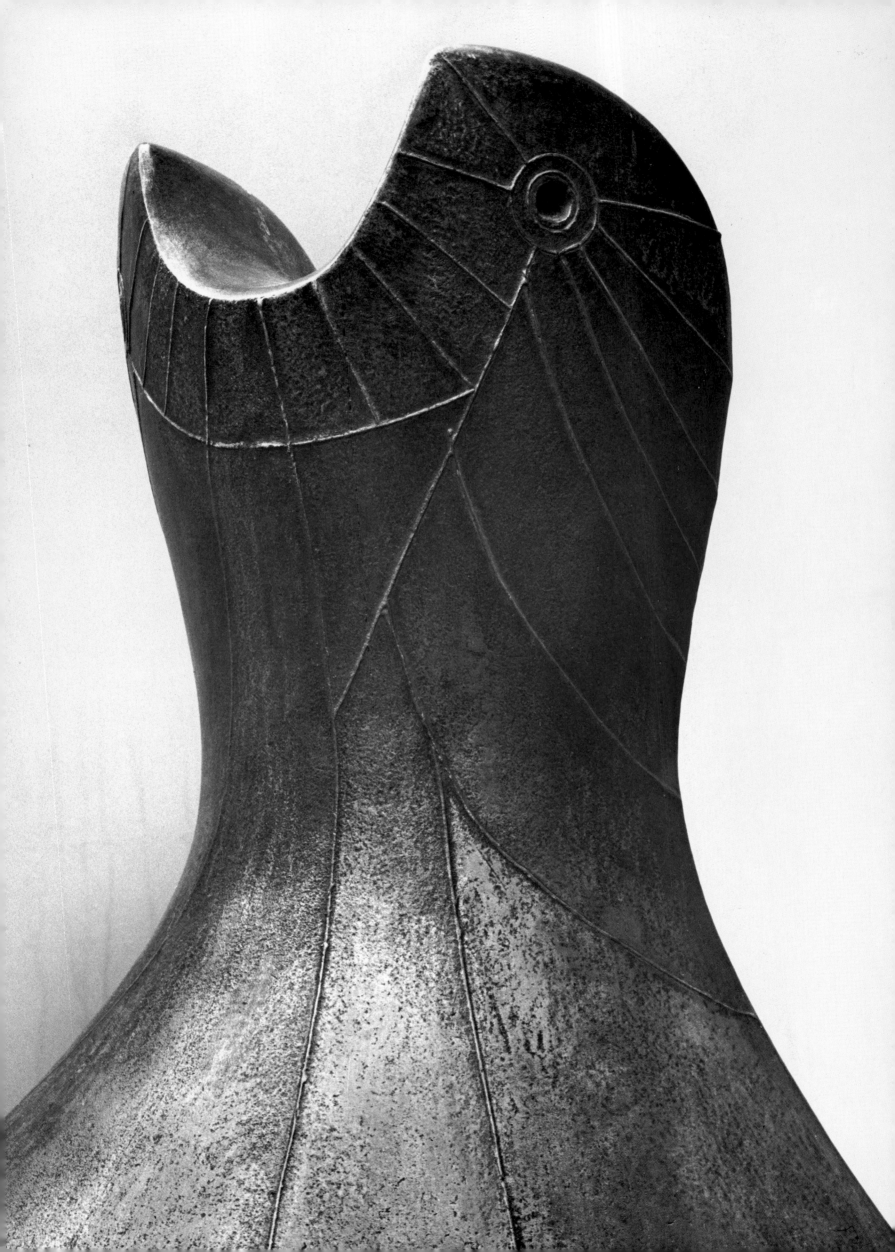

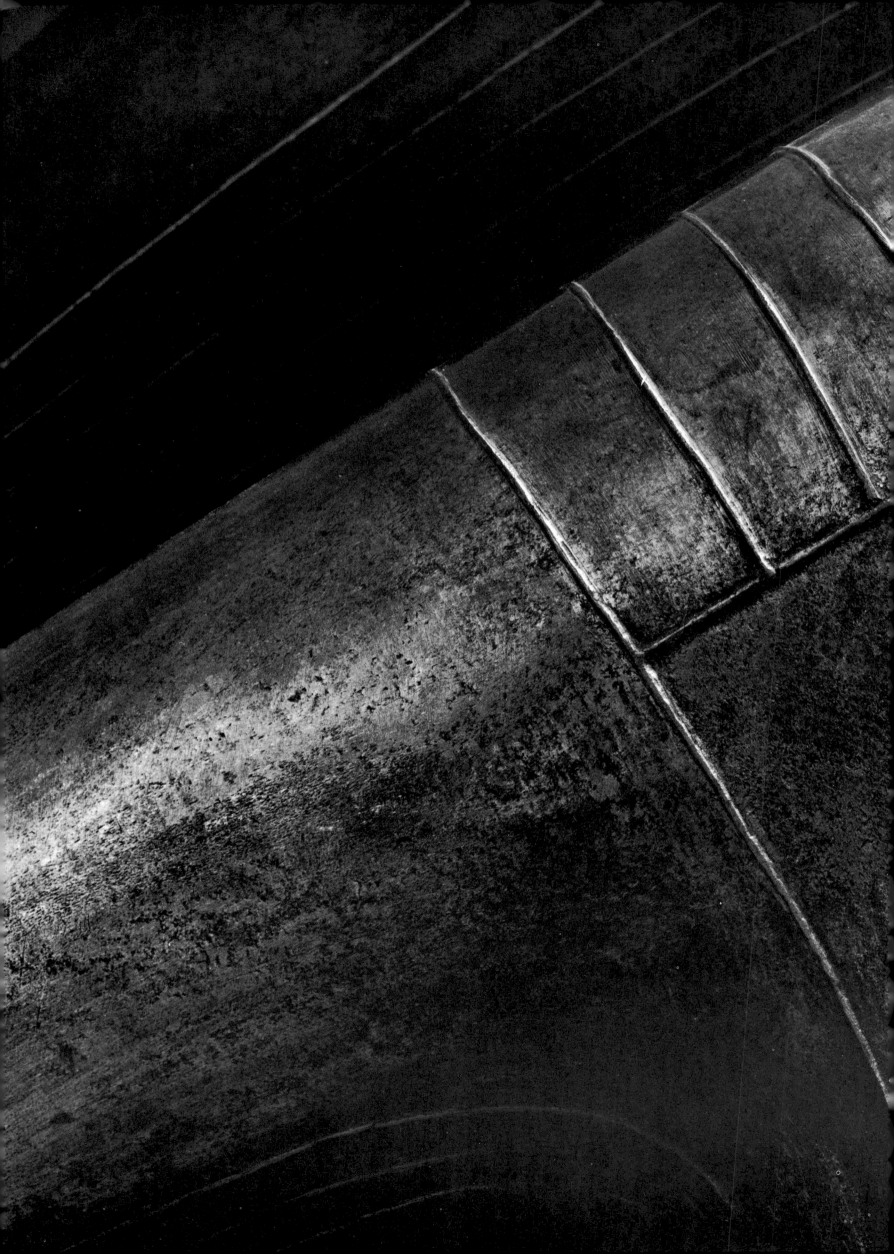

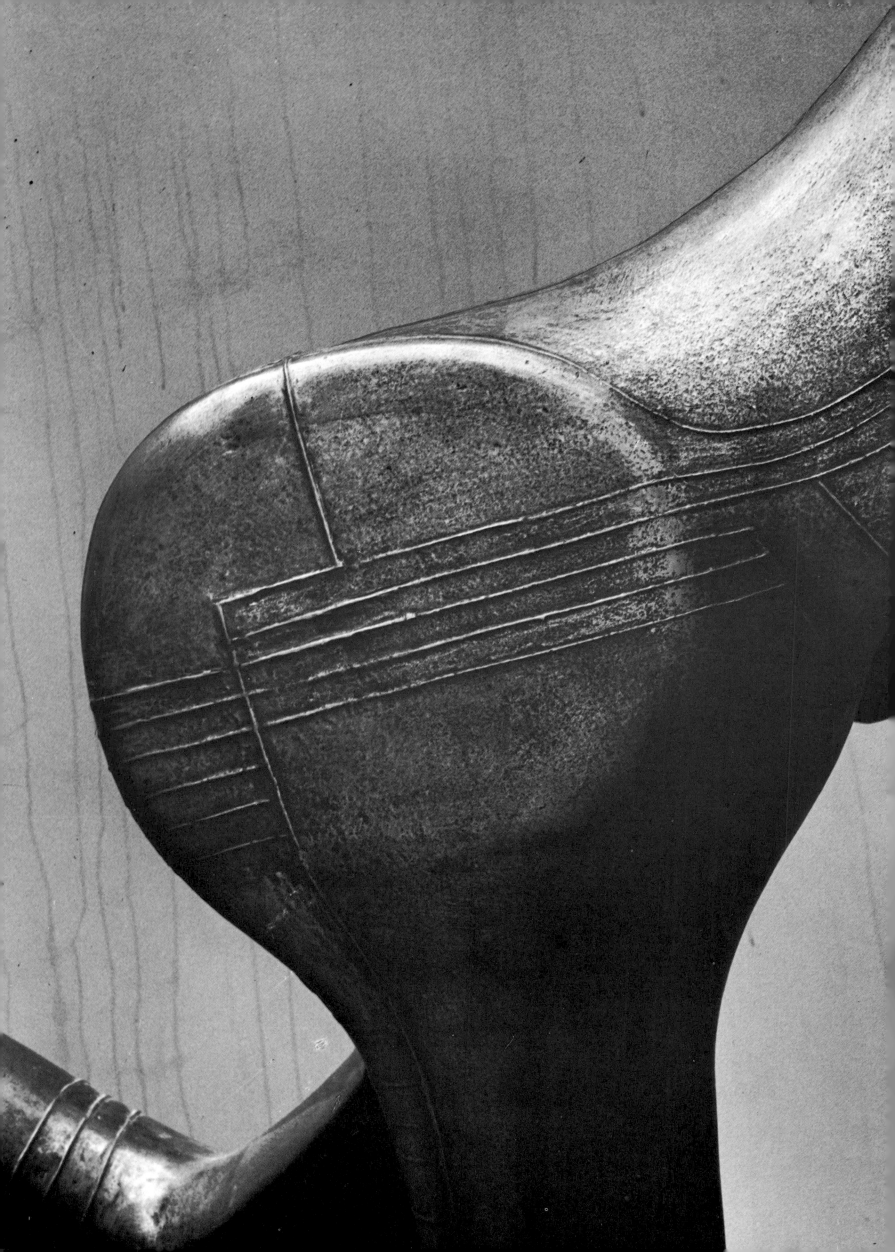

Certain of my works are more important to me than others, and I tend to look on them as keys to a particular period. Ones I can quickly pick out are the 1938 "Reclining Figure" in Hornton stone, in the Tate Gallery; the large elmwood 1939 "Reclining Figure", now in the Detroit Museum; the 1951 Festival "Reclining Figure", in bronze on the previous pages; and my first large bronze two-piece "Reclining Figure".

In addition the "King and Queen" represents for me something rather special, as does the "Warrior with Shield", because it was the first single male figure I had made in sculpture.

Of later works, I think the 1960–61 "Reclining Mother and Child" is important. Obviously there are others.

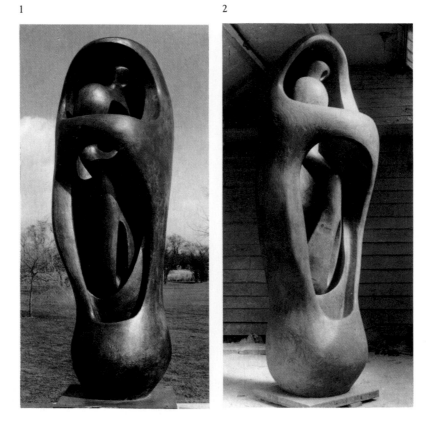

I have done other sculptures based on this idea of one form being protected by another. These are some of the helmets I did in 1939 in which the interior of the helmet is really a figure and the outside casing of it is like the armour by which it might be protected in battle. I suppose in my mind was also the Mother and Child idea and of birth and the child in embryo. All these things are connected in this interior and exterior idea. There were two versions of this sculpture, one in bronze and one in wood. Wood has a warmer, more human feel to it than bronze, but at the time I was unable to find the right piece of wood for it. I had intended that it should be somewhere around nine or ten feet high, and as I did not want the idea to go stale on me I began it in plaster some six or seven feet high. Eventually after having started the plaster version and nearly finished it, my timber merchant told me he had found a piece of elm wood that was suitable and so I used that for the second version.

This large reclining figure is called "External Form". The working model, right, has an interior piece, and in translating it into full size the internal form was also included. The two forms were, of course, made separately, although I continually fitted them together and related the shapes to each other. Later I decided the external form made a better sculpture on its own. The interesting result for me is that the interior form remains by implication.

3

4

5

6

Now we come to the "Reclining Figure" which was used for the terrace of the Time-Life building in Bond Street. Originally it wasn't for this purpose. Like all my sculptures it would have been done anyway. I had the idea for it and, in my opinion, it turned out about the right size and the right proportion for the Time-Life terrace. It is one of the earliest of my draped figures and must have been done just after my first visit to Greece which led to my doing the draped sculptures. My using drapery is a mixture of two happenings. Firstly there were the shelter drawings, which caused me to look at drapery and use drapery. Secondly the visit to Greece made me realise how the Greeks used drapery to emphasise the tension of the inside form. Of course I had previously studied draped sculpture in the British Museum, for example, the so-called "Three Graces". There, one has the projections of form from inside, the knees, the breasts, the shoulders pressing tightly outwards, and between these projections, the drapery falling more slackly in loose folds. So the pressure is emphasised from inside. This was how I tried to use drapery myself. I then began to see and to treat the drapery itself as a form element. The wrinkles and crinkles of the drapery at one stage began to remind me in close-up of mountain ranges.

This row of heads were try-outs for two sculptures for the local church. My great friend (and the patriarch of our village) asked me to do the sculptures after it was discovered that the two corbel heads on the arch of the porchway were not original but cement casts. As they were going to reconstruct the porch he thought it was a shame to put back what they knew were reconstructions when there was a sculptor living in the village. He asked if I would do them. I decided to carve a male head and female head and these were some of the models for them. I decided I was going to make them fit in with the old porch as best I could. I think they do.

In those days I didn't have an outdoor studio like I
have now, so the Time-Life screen had to be done
in front of the smaller studio next to the house.
I set the figures up at the distance they would be
apart when framed inside the screen of the Time-Life
building and, to see what they would look like from
a distance, I had to go on to the village green and
look over the hedge. The trouble was that I couldn't
see their backs, except from very close to. I intended
that each element should be pivoted so they could
be individually turned into varying positions on, for
example, the first day of every month. But it was
found to be impractical, because each block weighed
four or five tons, and it was thought they might be
a danger to the public. I still think it is a good idea
which could have been made safe and practical and
I hope to use it in some way in the future. It would
have the advantage of people not always seeing the
same view of a piece of sculpture in architecture.

No architectural site ever seems to be perfect. There
are always compromises to be made between the
sculpture and the architecture. When a sculpture is
put in a niche in a wall it can only be seen as a
frontal piece. My aim is to make sculpture which
is interesting from all angles. In my opinion you can
treat sculpture in relation to architecture, rather like
you treat pictures and sculpture inside a house. It
can be moveable, and fit into changing conditions.

I would like to buy back the Time-Life screen because
it looked so much better here in my garden than it
does in Bond Street, which is too narrow a street.

The four maquettes for the Time-Life building in Bond Street. First I tried to relate the openings to the fenestration of the building. This, I thought, was too obvious. Next I made more asymmetrical spaces and varied the size of each unit. But this had a rhythm too vertical for the squareness of the building. Then came the third, in which I used both horizontal and vertical forms and openings. Still I was dissatisfied. I made a fourth attempt which combined the horizontal and vertical forms into more squareness. I preferred this last maquette, and so carried it out in full size.

The five maquettes, on the right, are reliefs, but not for the Time-Life screen. The three horizontal ones are connected with the brick wall I made in Rotterdam. The two vertical reliefs are much earlier and were done in 1931.

214

7

8

9

In the maquette of the "King and Queen" I used a frame to
define the relationship of the two figures with the sense of
space outside them. From a side view, you can see more
easily that the King is sitting further back than the Queen
and that they are both turned to their left. However, when I
came to carry out the sculpture in its full size, the figures
looked as though they were sitting between goal posts. In
life size they didn't need the reference to an upright and a
horizontal, as the pose of each figure became obvious.

The head of the King is the clue to the whole sculpture . . .
A novelist, starting with a single incident or situation, can
construct the remainder of his novel from his knowledge of
life, his imagination and his art. The same thing happened
with this sculpture. The head of the Queen was a problem
because it had to be in harmony and I made two or three
different attempts at it before being satisfied.

All this reminds me of the delegation which came from
Antwerp to decide whether the city should acquire the
sculpture. I had been informed from Antwerp that it was
because there was opposition to its purchase that they were
sending some committee members to have a look at it. They
arrived in London during the terrible smog in 1953. They
were due at my studio at ten a.m. but by two o'clock in the
afternoon they had not arrived at Hoglands. As the fog was still
impenetrable, I gave them up and went back to work on the
"King and Queen". I was still unhappy with the head of the
Queen and decided to saw it off, thinking that I had time to
get it right. But sure enough, at 4 o'clock, still in dense fog,
the delegation arrived. They were so excited and proud of
themselves at having managed to reach me that they hardly
bothered to look at the sculpture. In fact, after a few minutes,
they realised they had better set off back to London or they
would never get home at all. When they had returned to
Antwerp all they could talk about was their terrible
experience. It was as if they had been to the North Pole.
When asked about the sculpture, they said, "Oh! that's all
right". And so the sculpture was bought.

The "King and Queen" is rather strange. Like many of my
sculptures, I can't explain exactly how it evolved. Anything
can start me off on a sculpture idea, and in this case it was
playing with a small piece of modelling wax. It was at a time
when I was thinking of starting my own bronze foundry.
I had a young sculptor assistant who was keen on the technical
side and wanted to know about casting bronze. I decided
to cut out the first stage, which would have meant making a
plaster cast, and to model directly in wax. Whilst
manipulating a piece of this wax, it began to look like a
horned, Pan-like, bearded head. Then it grew a crown and I
recognised it immediately as the head of a king. I continued,
and gave it a body. When wax hardens, it is almost as strong
as metal. I used this special strength to repeat in the body
the aristocratic refinement I found in the head. Then I
added a second figure to it and it became a "King and
Queen". I realise now that it was because I was reading stories
to Mary, my six-year-old daughter, every night, and most of
them were about kings and queens and princesses.
Eventually one of these sculptures went to Scotland, and is
beautifully placed by its owner, Tony Keswick, in a moorland
landscape. I think he rather likes the idea of the "King and
Queen" looking from Scotland across to England.

This standing figure, like a sentinel, with an echoing double-head, is beautifully placed on a natural outcrop of rock on this Scottish moor. The siting of all my sculptures at Glenkiln, Dumfries, is marvellously varied and is, to me, ideal. It proves why I prefer Nature to any other placing as a setting for my sculptures.

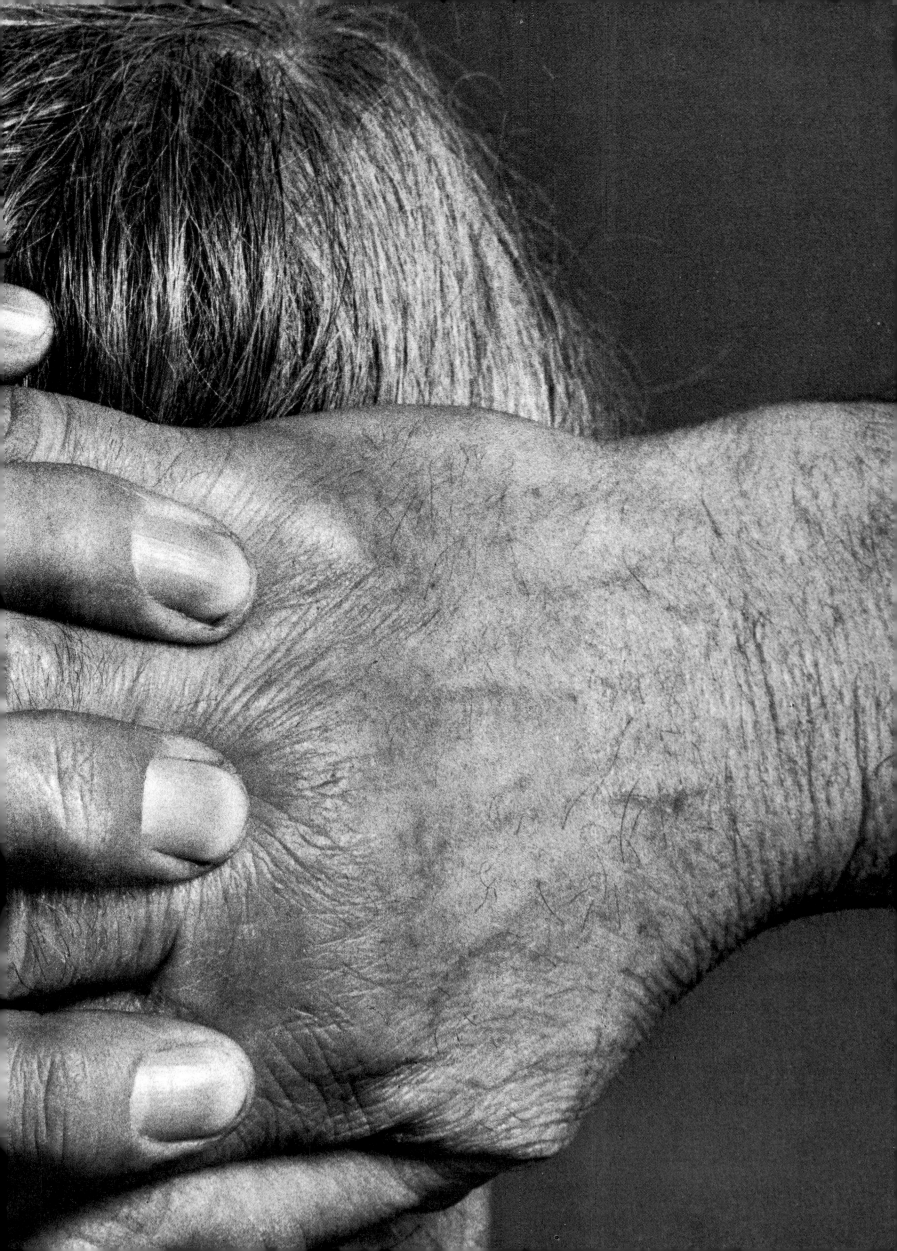

235

At Leeds School of Art in the first year I had drawn only from the male figure: in the provinces male models were all they could get. I remember the first time there was a female model—such terrific excitement, such novelty! All we had previously was the same Italian male model, who adopted all the set school-of-art poses, going through physical exercises with arms up, arms down and so on. I remember he had moustaches which you could see from the back.

The "Warrior with Shield" began when I found a small stone in the garden which reminded me of the stump of an amputated leg. I added to the pelvis, then made the chest, and gradually it grew from the stump into the whole figure. I became very involved in it, as of course I do in everything. But this was different. My excitement was due to the fact that, apart from being concerned with the male figure in my coal-mining drawings, this was the first single male figure I had done in sculpture since my student days. In working on the "Warrior with Shield", all the knowledge gained from the life drawing and modelling I had done years before came back to me with great pleasure.

"The Harlow Family Group." I had already done a small maquette
when the Harlow Arts Trust said that they would like a sculpture of
mine for Harlow New Town which was rehousing families from the
East End of London. A family group seemed to be most appropriate.
Actually it is to be re-sited because the present siting, although it is
quite good from my point of view, is too isolated. Children, out of
sheer naughtiness rather than viciousness, threw stones and fetched
pieces off the knee and nose and eventually knocked off the head of
the child. I have just repaired it, and it will go back to a more built-
up area where the children can be observed if they do any more
damage. It is a sculpture in Hadene stone. By this time my idea of
penetrating stone and cutting into it was much more free than it had
been some twenty years earlier. In my early days I wouldn't have carved
the large hole under the bench which the figures are sitting on, so that
you can see the legs from the back. But whilst it is more free, I have tried
to keep the formalised sense that it had been carved out of one block.
In feeling it is somewhat similar to "The Northampton Madonna."

The maquettes for this upright motif theme were triggered off for me by being asked by the architect to do a sculpture for the courtyard of the new Olivetti building in Milan. It is a very low horizontal one-storey building. My immediate thought was that any sculpture that I should do must be in contrast to this horizontal rhythm. It needed some vertical form in front of it. At the time I also wanted to have a change from the Reclining Figure theme that I had returned to so often. So I did all these small maquettes. They were never used for

the Milan building in the end because, at a later stage, when I found that the sculpture would virtually be in a car park, I lost interest. I had no desire to have a sculpture where half of it would be obscured most of the day by cars. I do not think that cars and sculptures really go well together. One of the upright motifs, without my knowing why, turned into a cross-form and is now in Scotland. We call it "The Glenkiln Cross", because the Glenkiln Farm Estate is where the first cast of it is placed. From a distance it looks rather like one of the old Celtic crosses.

My assistants are patinating the upright motifs, to give them the colour and surface quality I wanted. In my sculpture, whilst of course, colour counts, it's not the main thing. Otherwise I would have been a painter.

I often work in threes when relating things. Take the symbolic cross motif. I realised that, wherever it was placed with others, it had to be in the middle. When placed between two others, the three became a crucifixion group. The three of them are together as a group outside the Kröller-Müller Museum in Holland, and then there's another group of three in America, outside the Amon Carter Museum in Fort Worth. However, in Scotland I think the single cross is probably better placed: seen from across the moor your attention is drawn towards it as if X marks the spot. From a distance a cross form stands out so much more than any other form.

250

There's Mary at the time she was at Cranbourne Chase School. She wanted to improve her tennis. I remember we used to practise in the garden. . . . That's not a bad backhand of mine.

I started playing table tennis at the Royal College of Art. It was always very popular in the old Common Room. Some students became terrific experts. I still enjoy it very much and play often.

This scene in our garden has the quiet, subdued sensitivity of a Ben Nicolson painting; all delicate and pale.
The birds remind me of a late Braque. I have always been fascinated by birds. Birds' bones are the strongest and yet the lightest of all bones.

Unlike the lines on the figure for the Festival of Britain, that were produced by sticking thin strings onto the original plaster model and then casting them so that they came out as ridges, the lines on this head were produced by making a mould, and incising the lines into the plaster surface with a sharp metal point. The lines are transformed into ridges because from a mould you get the reverse when cast. It is a technique that I've used sculpturally to emphasise a projection, by drawing lines round the projection so that they gradually disperse in order that the eye is drawn to a focal point. If I want to show that a surface is coming in and going out, I draw a line on it for the eye to follow. Similarly, in some of my drawings I have used imaginary sectional lines, going down and across forms to show their shape, without the aid of light and shade. I could have developed this idea more than I have done in sculpture and perhaps, one day, I might come back to it with a different interpretation.

I like this little studio. I am always very happy there. I like the disarray, the muddle and the profusion of possible ideas in it. It means that whenever I go there, within five minutes I can find something to do which may get me working in a way that I hadn't expected and cause something to happen that I hadn't foreseen.

When I make a small maquette, it is rather like an architect making a sketch for a building on an envelope. In his mind it is a full-size building. In the same way, with my small plaster maquettes, I am thinking of something much larger. By looking at a maquette close to, I can relate it to some distant object and imagine it as huge. It's all a question of mental scale and not physical size.

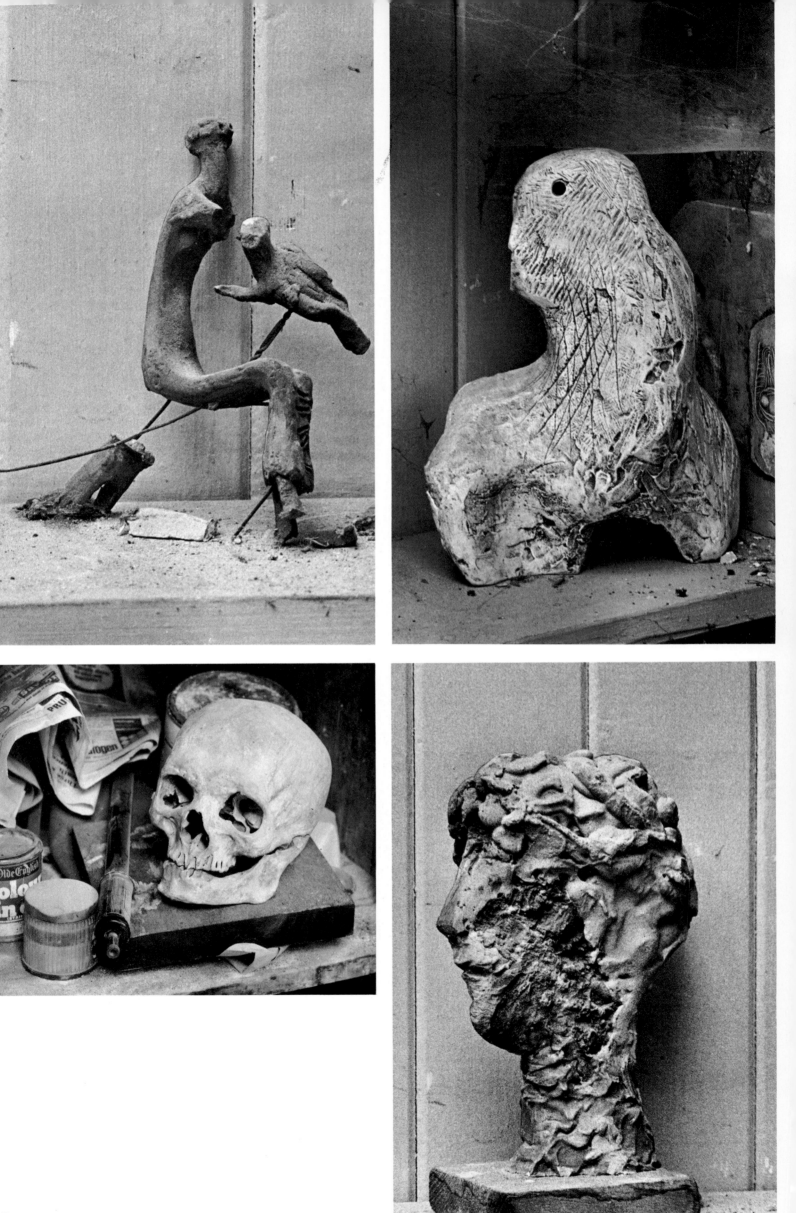

Because now I am aiming at sculpture that is truly three-dimensional, I want it to vary from whatever angle I look at it. Although it is a unified idea, it is not symmetrical. To explain its shape by drawing I should require at least twenty or thirty drawings. At one time, when my ideas were more frontal, I would often start a sculpture from an idea I'd produced in a single drawing and work out what was to happen at the sides and at the back as I went along, but, with the kind of sculpture I do now, I need to know it from on top and from underneath as well as from all sides. And so I prefer to work out my ideas in the form of small maquettes which I can hold in my hand and look at from every point of view.

A series of maquettes . . . only about one out of twenty ever gets translated into a bigger size. I doubt whether there is more than one here that I carried out in its intended full size.

The maquette for a wall in Rotterdam.
I wanted some elements to project
from the wall instead of all of it being
in flat relief. Because of the normal size
of a brick, it was necessary to make
some parts in high relief.

I didn't, of course, do the bricklaying myself.
I was told that the Dutch bricklayers were
tremendously clever and, no matter what
technical problems I gave them, they would
enormously enjoy trying to solve them. I went
over to Rotterdam and we did an experimental
piece together working out one of the forms in
its full size. It was quite a technical feat. To
me the final result of the finished wall was only
relatively satisfactory. It would have been
better if it had been a south wall facing the
sun. As it is, it only gets the sunlight for a
short while each day, which is a pity because
a relief needs a side light to look its best.

274

In the "Falling Warrior" sculpture I wanted a figure that was still alive. The pose in the first maquette was that of a completely dead figure and so I altered it to make the action that of a figure in the act of falling, and the shield became a support for the warrior, emphasising the dramatic moment that precedes death.

I turned this horizontal bronze figure into an upright wooden one. Although, of course,
I changed it considerably, it shows the great importance of gravity in sculpture.
Lying down, the figure looked static, whilst upright it takes on movement, and because
it is working against gravity it looks almost as though it is climbing.

At one time I thought I would make the Unesco sculpture in bronze. In a city, because of the impurities in the atmosphere, bronze always tends to become dark, and later I realised that the background to the sculpture would also be dark because the Unesco building stands on pilotti. So I made several maquettes, putting in my own background behind the figure. However, later I decided to use light coloured stone, and the background became unnecessary because the stone stood out against the darkness under the pilotti.

Using a wall with sculpture presented some interesting problems. In some cases I only used part of a wall and in others I used steps to make a setting. To give people looking at the sculpture from inside the building an inkling that there was something on the other side of the sculptured wall I made holes and cut-outs so that they would want to come and look at it from the front.

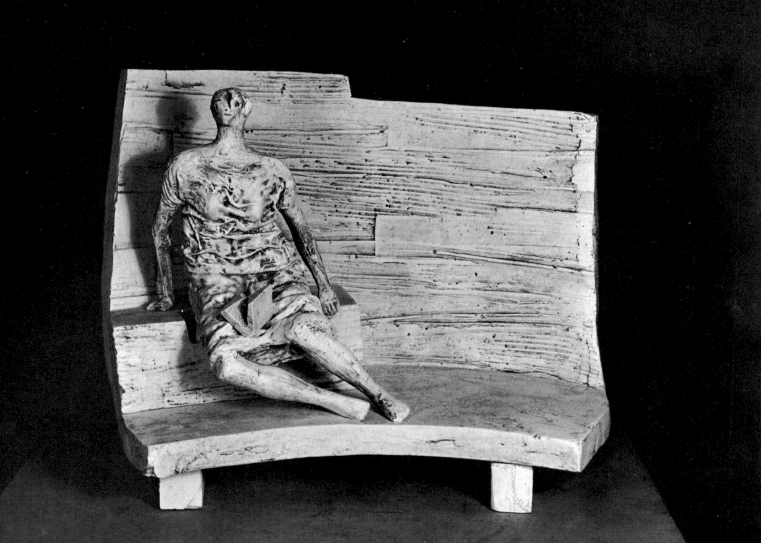

I knew that the big, draped, seated figure was going to be shown out of doors and this created the problem that the folds in the drapery could collect dirt and leaves and pockets of water. I solved it by making a drainage tunnel through the drapery folds between the legs. I found that using drapery in sculpture was a most enjoyable exercise in itself.

The way that this sculpture sits on the trolley gives me a fresh feeling and impression of it. When I saw her muffled, tied up, with a bandaged arm and on wheels, she became a living person for whom I felt sorry.

A sculpture of a nude, covered with snow, makes me feel uncomfortable, for I identify myself with a sculpture and am concerned with its physical context. Not only do I identify myself with my figurative pieces, but also with my more abstract works. For me there is always an organic human relationship with them somewhere below the surface.

I like using plaster as the preliminary material for my bronzes. When people talk about "truth to material" it doesn't strictly apply to bronze, because a sculptor does not take a solid piece of bronze and cut it into shape as he does a piece of stone. For a bronze, he first has to make his original in something else. The special quality of bronze is that you can reproduce with it almost any form and any surface texture through expert casting. However, if you desire to achieve the real metallic quality of bronze, it is necessary to work on the surface of the sculpture after it has been cast.

The advantage of using plaster is that it can be both built up, as in modelling, or cut down, in the way you carve stone or wood.

If you use clay it has to be kept in a malleable condition (if left untended for a week, it becomes hard and cracks), whereas you can leave plaster untouched indefinitely. To work on it again all you have to do is to soak it thoroughly in water, and then you can add further plaster to it as though you had only just left it for half an hour.

Although I like this piece, started in 1958, it has never been cast into bronze yet. I consider it to be nearly complete, but I am dissatisfied with the feet part. But there may come a time when I will go back to working on it. As a young sculptor, if I didn't finish a piece by continuously working on it, I would abandon it. But as I get older I can sustain my ideas longer. Now I can work on one piece intermittently, and over long periods, just as, for example, Cézanne worked on the late "Bathers" pictures for the last ten or fifteen years of his life, altering them throughout, as can readily be seen.

302

This "Seated Girl against Square Wall" is one of the ideas which I might have used for the Unesco sculpture. That was at the time when I thought of doing a very big bronze sculpture against a square wall. The spareness of her bony figure accentuates the articulation of her joints.

This is the bronze cast of the working model for the Unesco "Reclining Figure". The final stone sculpture is sixteen feet long and was easily the biggest sculpture I had done until then. As the original maquette was only six inches long I needed an intermediate working model, and so I made a plaster one-eighth in bulk of the final sculpture, and sent it to Italy, where I was to carve it in Roman travertine marble.

Some time after I had completed the stone sculpture, I cast the working model into bronze to preserve it, as there were differences between the two. This was just as well, as some time afterwards the plaster original was damaged. When carving, since one is cutting away and not building up as with plaster, there is always a tendency for the sculpture to be more bulky and squarified.

Roman travertine marble is a stone that I have loved ever since I first used it in 1932. I like its colour and its rough, broken, pitted surface. Knowing these characteristics I did not give the plaster working model a smooth surface. It was the first big stone sculpture that I had done since the Northampton "Mother and Child". I am quite satisfied that the sculpture is the right size, scale, and material for the building. Recently they have had to add to the building, and as the site could not be enlarged, the only way they were able to do it was to excavate an area in front of the sculpture and build some offices below ground level. I am told that this alters the previous relationship of the sculpture with the building.

The whole of my development as a sculptor is an attempt to understand and realise more completely what form and shape are about, and to react to form in life, in the human figure, and in past sculpture. This is something that can't be learnt in a day, for sculpture is a never-ending discovery.

When Michelangelo said that sculpture could express everything, he did not mean that sculpture could replace the functions of all the other arts, or that sculpture could play a banjo! He meant that it can express so much that you don't need to worry about what it can't do. In that sense it was enough for him . . . it is enough for twenty lifetimes.

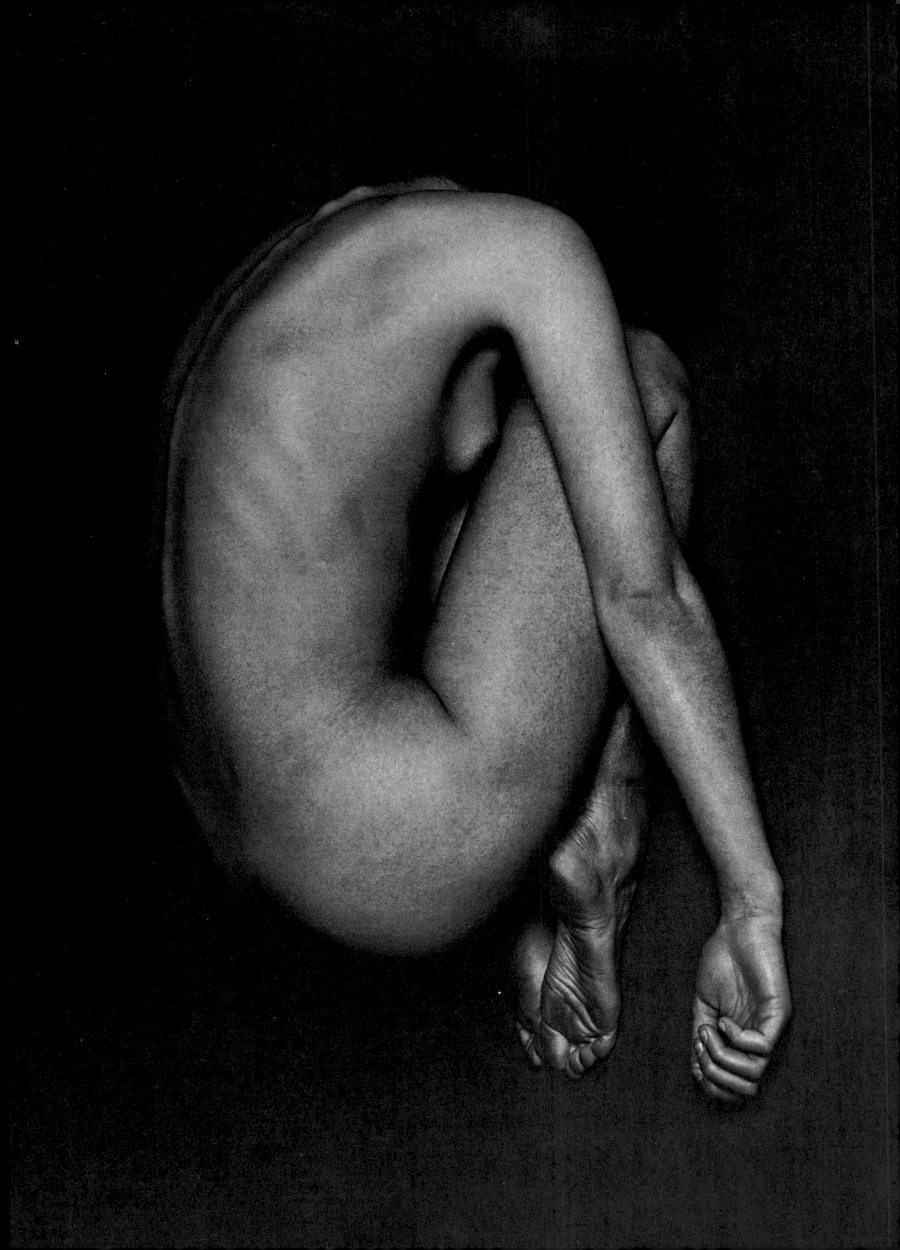

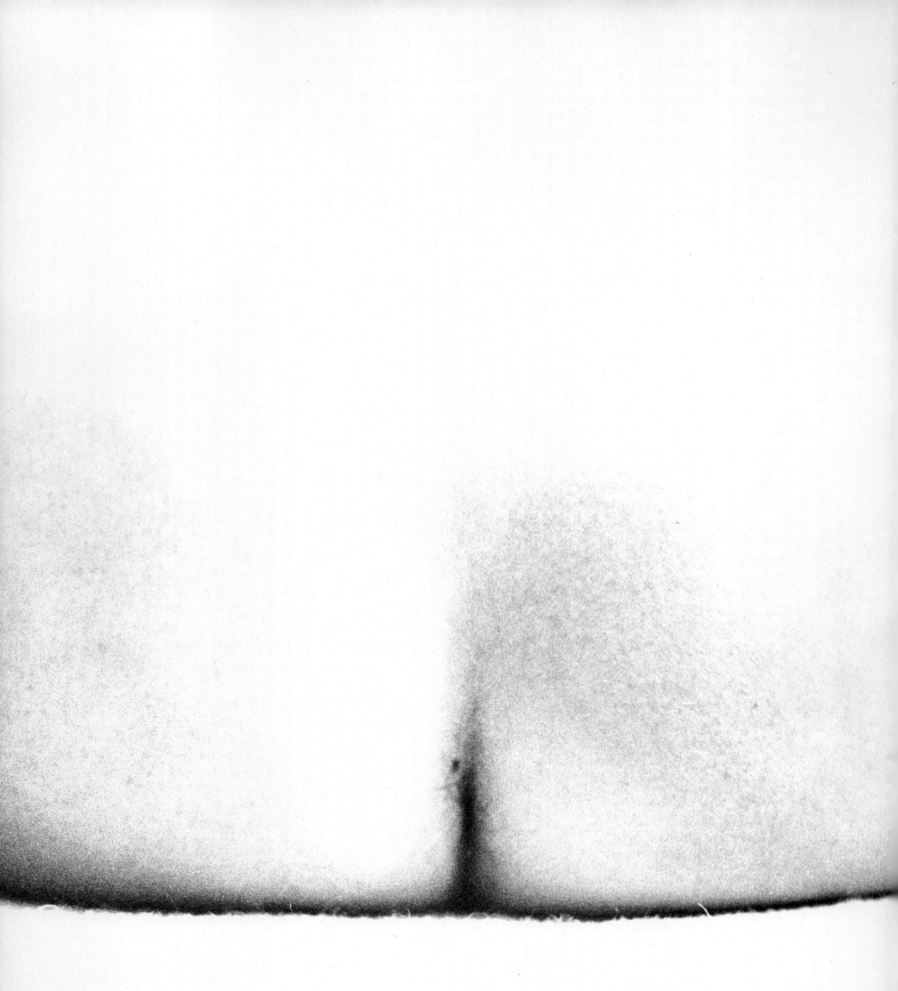

Right from the beginning I have been more interested in the female form than in the male. Nearly all my drawings and virtually all my sculptures are based on the female form. "Woman" has that startling fullness of the stomach and the breasts. The smallness of the head is necessary to emphasise the massiveness of the body. If the head had been any larger it would have ruined the whole idea of the sculpture. Instead the face and particularly the neck are more like a hard column than a soft goitred female neck.

"Woman" and "Seated Woman", opposite, both have the big form that I like my women to have. "Woman" emphasises fertility like the Paleolithic Venuses in which the roundness and fullness of form is exaggerated.

"Seated Woman", particularly her back view, kept reminding me of my mother, whose back I used to rub as a boy when she was suffering from rheumatism. She had a strong, solid figure, and I remember, as I massaged her with some embarrassment, the sensation it gave me going across her shoulder blades and then down and across the backbone. I had the sense of an expanse of flatness yet within it a hard projection of bone. My mother's back meant a lot to me.

One of Berenson's greatest tenets about art was this tactile quality. When we feel pain in our bodies we instinctively know where it is. This is a knowledge of form.

"Seated Woman" is pregnant. The fullness in her pelvis and stomach is all to her right. I don't remember that I consciously did it this way, but I remember Irina telling me, before Mary was born, that sometimes she could feel that the baby was on one side and sometimes on the other.

This "Reclining Figure" in elmwood took a long time to finish because in the early stages there was a crack in the lower part of it which hadn't shown itself in the large original tree trunk. I got somewhat disheartened when I found that this crack was getting bigger, and for a period I stopped working on it. However, the splitting slowed down, and eventually I took it up again and finished it. But from beginning to end it took me five or six years. I think the sculpture gained by having a slow evolution.

I like working with elmwood because its big grain makes it suitable for large sculptures, and because of the cool greyness of the wood. An interesting point about working with wood is that it must come from a live tree. Dead wood, by which I mean wood from a tree that has died, has no qualities of self-preservation and rots away.

Isaac Witkin, my assistant at the start of the sculpture, liked carving and was very helpful on the "roughing out" of this sculpture. With a big tree trunk there is so much preliminary work that so long as I am around to supervise, a competent carver can do the early shaping, allowing me to get on with something else. I take over for the final stages which cannot be hurried. Finishing a large wood sculpture is like a nibbling mouse gnawing a hole in a wall.

It's a sculpture that I continue to be fond of. Besides that, it's the only large wooden one left in England. The others are all in the U.S.A. The seven foot long "Reclining Figure" in elmwood carved in 1939 is in Detroit. There is one in the Cranbrook Academy of Art, Michigan, another large one in the Guggenheim Museum, and a fourth in the Albright-Knox Gallery, Buffalo. This one I want to keep in England.

I have always been excited about natural strata and the actual forms of stone. Photographs of places such as the Grand Canyon, the rocky coast of Brittany and big, natural rocks in river beds have always excited me. I have often drawn rock strata and been influenced by its formations.

My "Two-Piece Reclining Figure Number One" of 1959 is a mixture of rock form and mountains combined with the human figure. I didn't reason it out like this, but I think that this is the explanation. Breaking it in half made it a less obvious, a less realistic figure. In the maquette the leg and the head end were joined but when I came to enlarge the sculpture there was a stage when the junction between the leg and head didn't seem necessary. Then I realised that dividing the figure into two parts made many

more three-dimensional variations than if it had just been a monolithic piece.

This was something I'd wanted to do in sculpture for a long time. It led on to several other two-piece sculptures and eventually to a three-piece one. As early as 1932 I had divided figures up into two, three or four parts, and so this wasn't an entirely new thing for me, but now I was using the space more sculpturally than I had earlier.

The leg end began to remind me as I was doing it of Seurat's "Le Bec du Hoc", which Kenneth Clark owned. I had seen it on numerous occasions and have always admired it tremendously.

I always want a sculpture that's given me a lot of trouble to turn out better than one that has been less worry, but it doesn't necessarily mean that it does. Undoubtedly, time

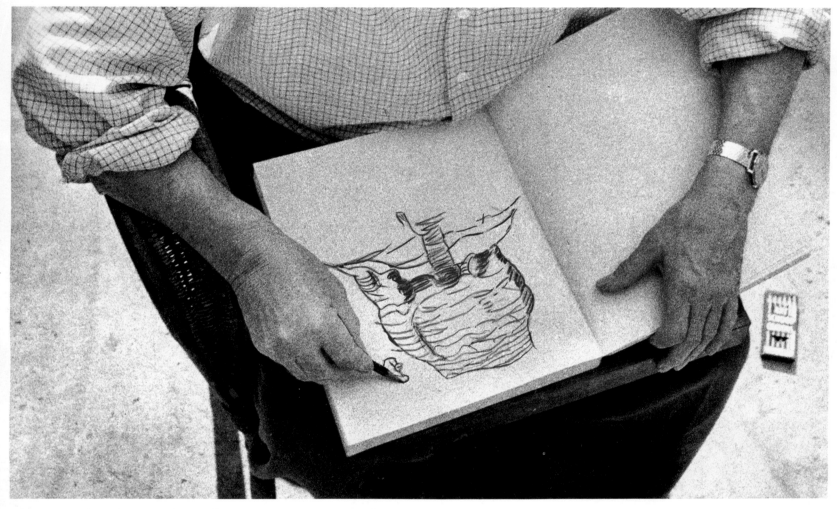

spent does show in a work. I think a sculpture that has forty days of your life in it should, in consequence, have more to it than a piece that has been thrown off in half an hour.

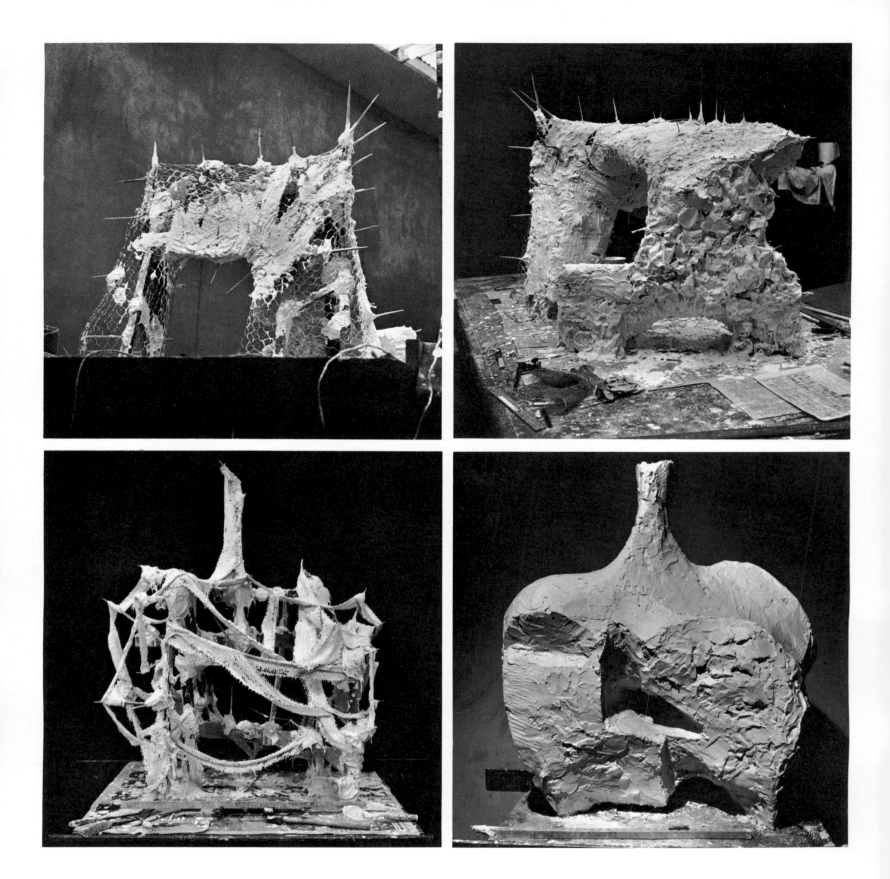

This is how my plaster originals grow. At one time I used wire netting in making the armature, but this caused immense trouble when I made alterations which are always necessary in enlarging the maquette into a full size sculpture. Now for the armature I use only wood struts and scrim, a form of open-work sacking.

The leg end, above, of the Reclining Figure Number Two "Two-Piece" began to remind me, towards its completion, of Monet's painting of the "Cliff at Etretat". I kept thinking of this arch as if it was coming out of the sea. This is the figure which led to me agreeing to make the Lincoln Center sculpture which stands in water.

"Two-Piece Reclining Figure Number Two." At first I used
to have a tremendous shock going from the white plaster
model to the finished bronze sculpture. But after twenty-five
years of working in plaster for bronze I can now visualise what
is going to happen. The main difference is that bronze takes
on a density and weight altogether unlike white plaster. For
example, look at the plaster on the previous page compared
with the finished bronze. The plaster has a ghost-like unreality
in contrast to the solid strength of the bronze. If I am not
absolutely sure of what is going to happen when the white
plaster model is cast into bronze, I paint it to make it look
like bronze. After a sculpture is cast it's too late, of course, to
make any big alterations.

Making a sculpture in two pieces means that, as you walk
round it, one form gets in front of the other in ways you
cannot foresee, and you get a more surprising number of
different views than when looking at a monolithic piece. The
space between the two parts has to be exactly right. It's as
though one was putting together the fragments of a broken
antique sculpture in which you have, say, only the knee, a
foot and the head. In the reconstruction the foot would have
to be the right distance from the knee, and the knee the right
distance from the head, to leave room for the missing parts—
otherwise you would get a wrongly proportioned figure. So,
in these two-piece and three-piece sculptures the space
between the pieces is a vital part of the sculpture.

349

"Three-Part Object" is a strange work, even for me. Three similar forms are balanced at angles to each other. In my mind it has a connection with insect life, possibly centipedes. Each segment has a leg, and there is an element in the sculpture nearer to an animal organism than a human one.

351

There is a difference between literary criticism and art criticism in the sense that literary critics are working in their own medium. In their literary criticism, Baudelaire, Coleridge and Eliot really knew what they were about because they were poets, whereas very few art critics are practising artists. Therefore they are more inclined to make stupid errors. In art criticism I entirely agree with Dr Samuel Johnson as quoted below.

An artist should not be controlled by the opinions of critics. With friends it may be different. For example, I ask Irina whether she thinks certain drawings or sculptures should be sent to one exhibition or another. Again, I might ask friends such as Herbert Read or Kenneth Clark which idea out of several drawings they think is better for a certain project. But I wouldn't ask either of them whether they think I should follow a certain direction or not, or how I should do a certain sculpture. A painter might ask his framer for advice on the framing of a picture, but he would never ask how to paint the picture.

Too much art criticism is advice to change the work of art in the direction the critic recommends. I don't say that an artist should not listen to other people's opinions, only that he doesn't have to take any notice of it.

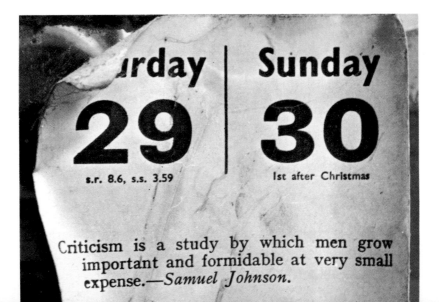

arday | **Sunday**

29 | **30**

s.r. 8.6, s.s. 3.59 | 1st after Christmas

Criticism is a study by which men grow important and formidable at very small expense.—*Samuel Johnson.*

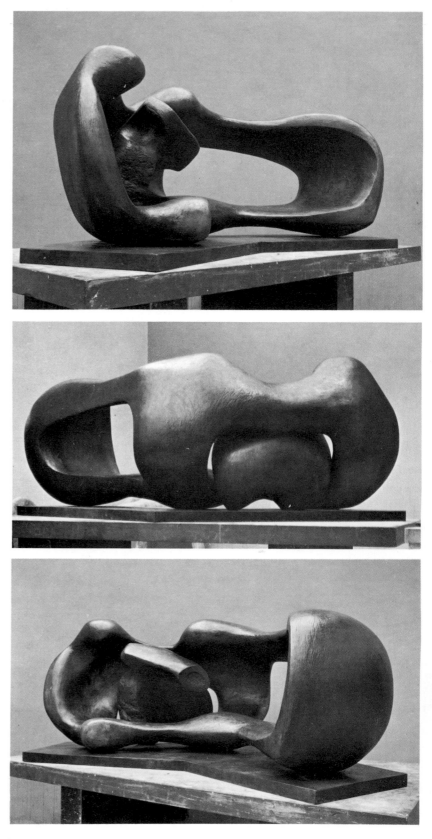

I have a particular liking for this "Reclining Mother and Child". (The beginning of the plaster original can be seen on the left of the previous page.) This work combines several of my different obsessions in sculpture. There's the reclining figure idea; the mother and child idea; and the interior-exterior idea. So it is the amalgamation of many ideas in one sculpture.

The contrast of these two heads shows that facial features are not essential for expression. With her long neck, one is distant and proud while the other is more sympathetic.

From some views, the thinness of the neck and head in the torso figure gives to the body an expansiveness I wanted whilst, from other views, the neck has a more normal width. "Standing Figure: Knife Edge" is a sculpture based on the principle wherein the thinness of one view contrasts surprisingly with the width of another. It was my liking for bones that led me to using the sharp edge, and in fact I included a fragment of a real bone in producing the maquette, on page 360, for the figure.

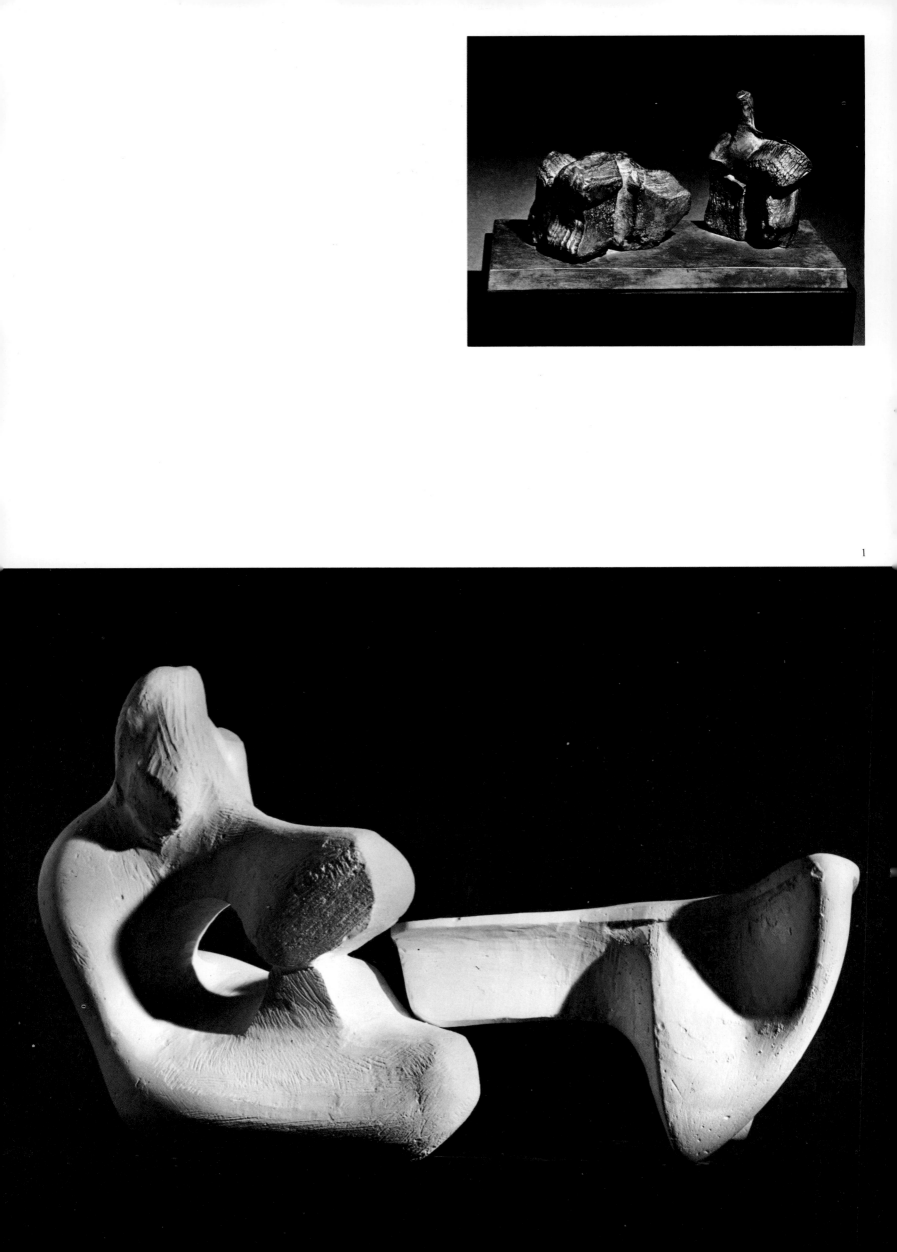

The sculpture below is the so-called "Tortoise Form". It is one right-angled form, repeated five times, and arranged together to make an organic composition. This repeated slow right-angle reminded me of the action of a tortoise. I think I shall pursue the idea of using a repetitive unit in some future works.

The plaster, on the opposite page, is the maquette for the large "Two-Piece Reclining Figure Number Nine", which is being cast into bronze in Berlin at this moment.

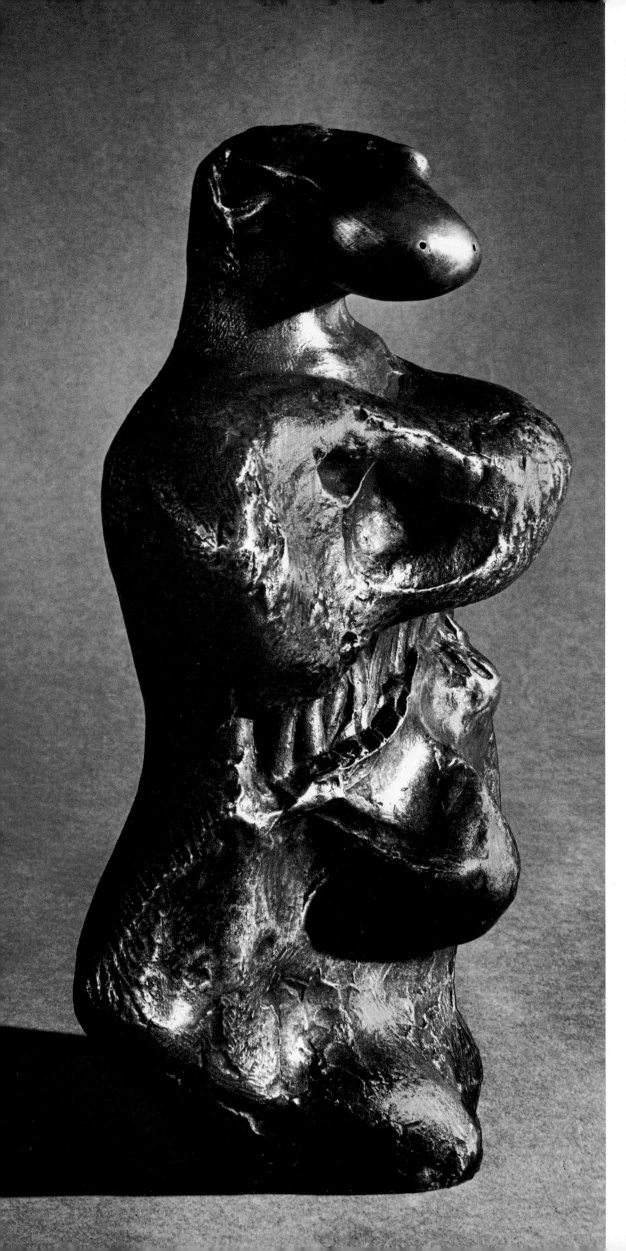

This piece with a head is rather like a hippopotamus and reminds me a little of some white plaster casts of seated figures dating from the Neolithic period in the British Museum.

I was going to work further on the sculpture on page 368 and change its form. In order to add plaster to previous plaster, you cut and scratch the surface so that it keys in. However, I was temporarily distracted by other work, and when I came to look at it again, I decided to leave it as it was. The surface ripples on some shells inspired the idea of the drapery on the lower part of the figure on page 369.

This round form was used as one of the forms in "Three Motifs against Wall". It is a view which ordinarily isn't seen because this is the side facing the background wall.

These again are ideas which could have been carried out on a larger scale. There simply isn't time to realise in full size all my ideas.

1/2/3

4/5/6

The good thing about my exhibition at Whitechapel Gallery, which Bryan Robertson arranged and organised so well, was that, for the first time, I had thirty or more sculptures all in one room, rather than in several smaller rooms. I liked the fact that the Gallery is on ground level and opens straight onto the street, so that people are encouraged to come in. Women even brought their children in prams. This doesn't happen in many galleries.

I hate going to my own exhibitions once they are on, because I don't want to have to talk to people about my work. I can enjoy talking to individuals about sculpture at home or at dinner parties and at small private gatherings. To have the public eye, to feel that I have the public watching me with my sculpture—this is something that I dislike.

At one time I became very interested in doing my own bronze casting. I had an assistant then who was ambitious to be a bronze caster rather than a sculptor. So I built a little foundry at the bottom of the garden. And I am very glad I did, because I learnt much about the characteristics of bronze which has been very helpful to me ever since. However, after a year of doing my own casting, I found the amount of time being taken up doing technical jobs was preventing me from doing as much sculpture as I wanted. Besides, professional bronze casters could do the job better than I. Now I send all my sculpture away to be cast and visit the foundry several times during the process to make any necessary alterations.

I use a foundry in London (previous pages) for the medium- and life-size sculptures, but I now go to Noack in Berlin for the really big ones. I like a bronze to come back from the foundry clean and bright like a new penny. From then on it is possible, by the use of various chemicals, to give it a patina which helps its sculptural form. Bronze is a material which can be changed to any colour as well as being able to be highly polished. Clean air will turn it green, as seen on country church roofs. Nearer the sea the salt makes it greener still. In cities the smoke and carbon dioxide tend to make it black.

When working in plaster for bronze I need to visualise it as a bronze, because on white plaster the light and shade acts quite differently, throwing back a reflected light on itself and making the forms softer, less powerful . . . even weightless.

Sometimes I have to turn a large sculpture on its side and on its back. Actually I should do it more often, because the more varied the angles from which I can see a sculpture, the more I understand it and the more critical I am of something which is not working.

Of these two I only cast one into bronze because I was
dissatisfied with the other. The plaster one has not yet
satisfied me. The projecting parts are too evenly spread and
too evenly apportioned throughout the figure. There is no
obvious focal point. In the bronze sculpture you know the
middle and you know where the shoulders are. It has a centre,
a kernel, and an organic logic.

Irina loves the garden and she works as hard in it as I do in the studio. I give her practically no help, except perhaps now and then I wheel a heavy barrow to the rubbish dump. Irina has changed five acres of ground of barbed-wired chicken runs, rhubarb patches, piggeries, etc., into a simple and excellent setting for my sculpture, which is a great help and asset. Without that piece of ground I cannot imagine how I could have produced some of the large sculptures that I have done in the last ten years. If a large sculpture has to be made in a studio it would be impossible to get away from it, and I would tend to work on its surface rather than on its bigger architectural forms. In our garden I can place the sculptures and see what they look like from a distance and in all weather conditions.

This is one of the little bones that I picked up in the garden and from which I can find principles and ideas. It has a remarkable sense of rock and roughness. From objects like this, I have learnt to appreciate varieties and textures, even rhythms. For some reason there seem to be hundreds of bones in our garden. Some of them are very old—maybe some two hundred and fifty years old. The farmers in those days were often butchers as well.

From my student days I have always been interested in bone structure. The Natural History Museum was so close to the Royal College of Art that I spent much time there. The wonderful collection of bones with such a variety of structures was terribly exciting for me, particularly the pre-historic bones which had become fossilised almost into natural sculpture.

These pieces are natural wood in the state in which I found them. The one looking like the head of a deer is from the bed of a river and worn smooth by the running water, and the other like an opening flower I picked up in the coppice at the end of my garden. Two more examples of the "found object", Nature's sculpture.

On the far left is a "Mother and Child", modelled in clay. I made it some ten or fifteen years ago from a drawing. I don't now start my sculptures from drawings, preferring to begin them in plaster maquettes. The touching of the two stomachs is the main point of the sculpture. The mother and the child gain a kind of warm, human, fleshy feeling through this contact. This comes through in the terracotta, and, wanting to preserve it, I had it cast into bronze. But unfortunately, owing to the technical difficulty of casting deep recesses in bronze, the result lost a little of the warmth of the terracotta original. Next to it is a shape formed by modelling wax which had accidentally leaked out whilst being poured into a cracked mould. I kept it because it proved to me that certain natural objects must owe their form to the fact that they were once molten material.

The other two photographs each show how the placing of two flintstones together causes them to assume an animate relationship.

"Saw Edge" was meant to be realised some ten or twelve feet high but it never went beyond this maquette.

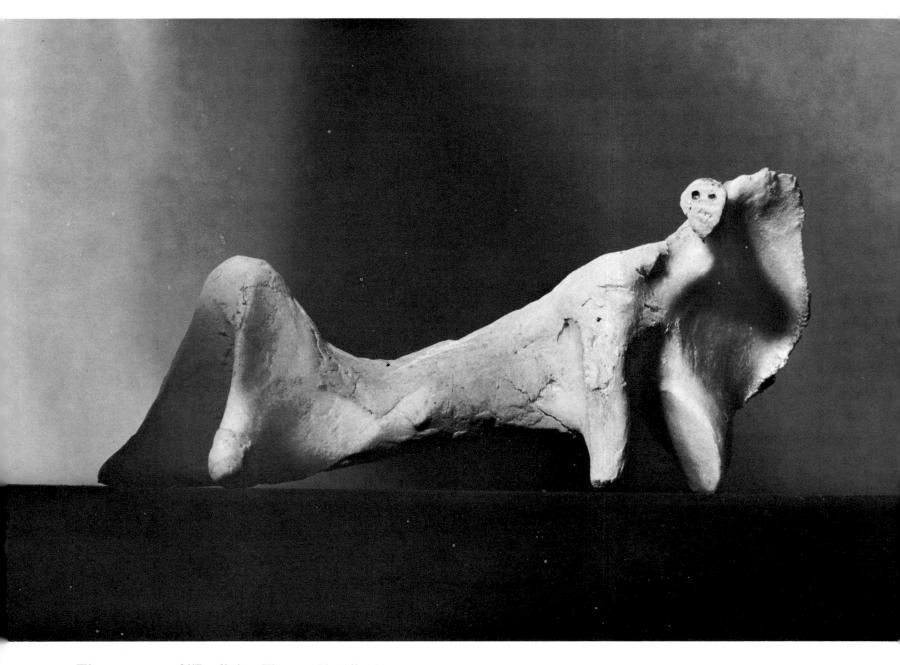

The maquette of "Reclining Figure: Cloak", above, was cast into bronze last year and is about fifteen inches long.

The titles of both the pieces here are purely descriptive.

I think this arch would have been better had I made it one foot taller, so that an average person could have walked through it, like through a doorway. As it is, you have to bend down slightly. This is because it was made in winter in the studio and I never saw it from far enough away to realise that the height was wrong.

With the "Reclining Figure: Bridge Prop", the prop is an arm supporting the figure. In making it, I was reminded of the view under Waterloo Bridge which I had passed on numerous occasions. The arches, seen from the Embankment, are strong.

2

3

4

5/6

Ten years ago I made a terracotta bird table. A big, black crow (I particularly like crows) used to come and eat from this table. I think it came because it was old and sick and it was the only way it could get its food. It had something wrong with its beak and it stood almost horizontally. That bird is why I did this sculpture.

7

8

Of course, when I come to make a sculpture two or three times life-size, continuous alterations have to be made. While a small object can be taken in at one glance, with a large object you have to move your eyes from the bottom to the top, and from side to side. A completely different perspective is physically involved. For example, the working model of the Lincoln Center sculpture was half-size i.e. just over seven feet high, while the finished sculpture was nearly fifteen feet high.

When I was working on the finished sculpture I found the perspective made the neck look shorter and the head look smaller. So I had to alter it to produce the same effect that I had achieved in the half-size working model. It all adds up to the fact that I react to the sculpture I'm doing through what I actually see. It's up to me as man-to-man with the sculpture.

We built a small swimming pool at Much Hadham for Mary, although she hardly ever swam in it. It was most useful, however, for trying out the Lincoln Center preliminary model and for working out its reflections in water.

This final sculpture in New York is still waiting for its proper level of water. I made the mistake of agreeing to the installation before the site was ready and the pool had been properly waterproofed and tiled. I knew of course that the sculpture was to stand in a large pool, and I was told its depth would be one foot two inches. Therefore in making the sculpture I allowed for its base to be submerged to that depth. In fact the water can never be that deep without it overflowing. I had had no previous experience of working on sculpture placed in water and as I have no control over the authorities, this mistake has not been put right. From the very outset the pool has never had more than six inches of water in it, sometimes much less. Even if it could be filled to a depth of one foot, it would look very much better. So far it has never been seen in the way that I planned it.

I have never taken holidays in the sense that I have gone away and not worked. As a young sculptor, my holidays were a time for feeling free to develop, to control my own direction and to express my own ideas rather than do exercises or examinations set by the College. As a result they were always very fruitful and interesting periods and I worked harder during my summer holidays both at the Leeds School of Art and at the Royal College of Art than I ever did in term time.

I first went to Querceta, near Forte dei Marmi in Italy, in connection with the Unesco sculpture. Querceta is a little village which lies beneath the mountain called Altissimo, part of the famous marble mountain range behind Carrara. Altissimo is for me a most fascinating and exciting place. It is where Michelangelo spent two years of his life quarrying marble. Altissimo is owned by a firm called Henraux, who deal in stone from all over the world. It was they who supplied the Roman travertine which was used on the Unesco building in Paris and, when I decided that the Unesco sculpture was to be a carving and not a bronze, it seemed right to use the same stone. The Unesco sculpture was to be so big that the cost of sending the stone to England would have swallowed up the whole of my fee. Therefore I went to the mountain, instead of the mountain being sent to me. To do the Unesco sculpture meant that I was in Italy intermittently for nearly a year. I would go over for three or four weeks, work on the stone and, because I hated being away from home and from Irina and Mary, who was then only a child, I would come home for a month and then go back again. Whilst I was in England, I would leave the straightforward roughing out of the stone to two of Henraux's stonemasons.

On some of these visits Irina and Mary came with me. It was a holiday for them, being so near the sea, and because they enjoyed it so much, after the Unseco sculpture was finished we continued to go there every year for two or three weeks. I find I have become so used to working continuously that, after a week off, I am conscience-stricken and I stop enjoying myself. The solution is to go to Henraux's and do a bit of carving each morning.

Three years ago an Italian painter friend sold me his cottage and now the three of us can go to Italy every summer for at least two months. Irina and Mary have a lovely holiday, and I work in the mornings and join them in the afternoons for the Italian sunshine and warm bathing.

417

On the Beach

Teaching Sebastian to swim
Hedgecoe

Playing
with
Dolly
& Sebastian

HM's feet.

Resting after picnic lunch
on beach.

Mary & me

at Forte dei Marmi

Demonstrating to Dolly + Sebastian

A good leap.

legs of H.M.

Back view of H.M.

Dolly objecting to being dipped by her mother + H.M.

420

Mary and I are very close. She doesn't let me put on false
dignities and I am glad. She has a great sense of fun.

Forte dei Marmi has changed a great deal. When I first went, there was hardly anybody on the beach. Now in summer it is rather crowded. But we don't mind this so much, for in England we live quietly in the country at Much Hadham, and don't lead a very social life.

Originally I had intended having a studio at the cottage, but because handling large pieces of stone is very difficult, I find that it is much easier to work in a room given to me in Henraux's stone-yard, where I can have all the facilities of their cranes. So what was to have been my studio has become my sleeping quarters for any of Mary's friends who visit us in the summer.

Our routine every day is to get up around seven-thirty, have a very simple breakfast in the garden of coffee and fruit. I try to get to Henraux's not later than ten and work until one o'clock, before joining Irina and Mary on the beach. I can be with them by ten past one and have my morning bathe. We leave the beach probably by quarter to two and do whatever shopping there may be. By three we have finished lunch and, following the Italian custom, we take it easy until four-thirty or five. Just occasionally I go back to the stone-yard for an hour or two. At other times, I may do a little drawing in my sketch book. In the evening we go out for a meal. These months in Italy always pass very quickly.

Last year I would have been quite happy to stay on an extra two or three weeks rather than face all the correspondence, etc., I knew was waiting for me at home. Nevertheless, I am usually very pleased to be back at Hoglands. My roots are in England and going abroad makes me appreciate it all the more.

As you go through this
apparently Gothic
entrance into one of
Henraux's quarries, it is
like passing down the
knave of a great
cathedral. In the
beginning the top was
merely an arched
passage and over the
years, as the marble has
been dug out of the
quarry beyond, the
floor has been dropped
until the roof is now
over sixty feet high.

In spite of all Henraux's modern cranes and cutting machinery there is still an important role for the horse in moving the smaller pieces of marble.

This "Mother and Child", in rosa aurora marble, which I completed last summer is made out of two blocks to fit together. I finished it at the same time as "Sculpture: Hole with Light", in soraya travertine marble, on page 441.

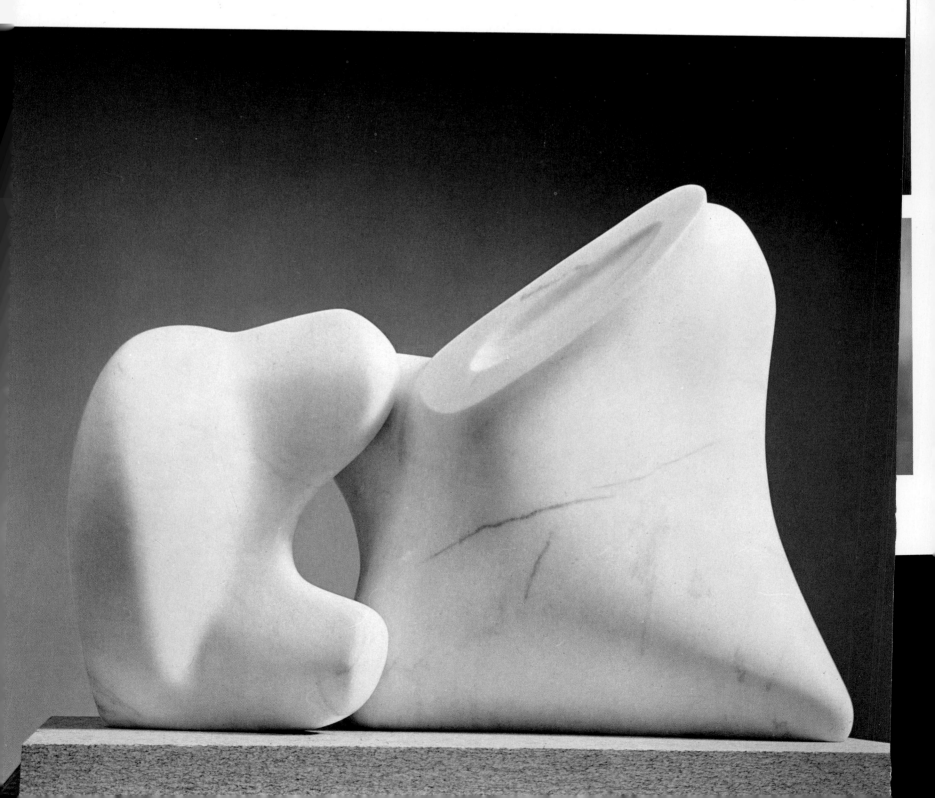

I am by nature a stone-carving sculptor, not a modelling sculptor. I like chopping and cutting things, rather than building up. I like the resistance of hard material. At one time I used to think that a stone sculpture was superior to a modelling, but I don't think so any more, since it is the quality of the final result which counts, no matter how it is made. Even now, in producing my bronzes, the process that I use in making the plaster original is a mixture of modelling and carving.

The marvellous thing about my cottage in Italy is that every year, I can live there and work in stone, the material that I like most.

Now that I am doing carving again, it is natural that the carvings I did between 1920 and 1940, a period in which perhaps nine out of every ten sculptures I made were carvings, have influenced the work I am doing now. So in carving I am picking up, as it were, where I left off.

And yet in spite of the connection, my present stone carvings are less restricted. Whilst I still believe in keeping a stone quality, I am not as afraid of hurting the stone or damaging it as I used to be. Hence there is more freedom in my compositional ideas.

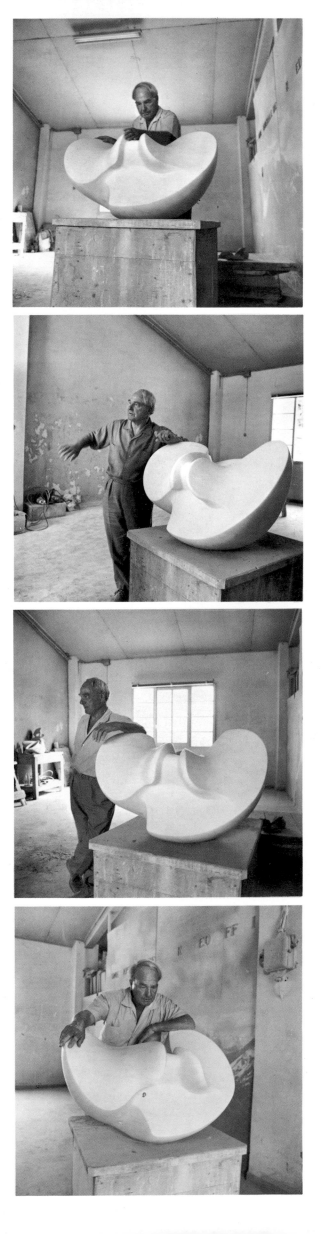

"Locking Piece" is certainly the largest and perhaps the most successful of my "fitting-together" sculptures. In fact the two pieces interlock in such a way that they can only be separated if the top piece is lifted and turned at the same time.

The germ of the idea originated from a sawn fragment of
bone with a socket and joint which was found in the
garden. Given this theme, I made the complete sculpture.

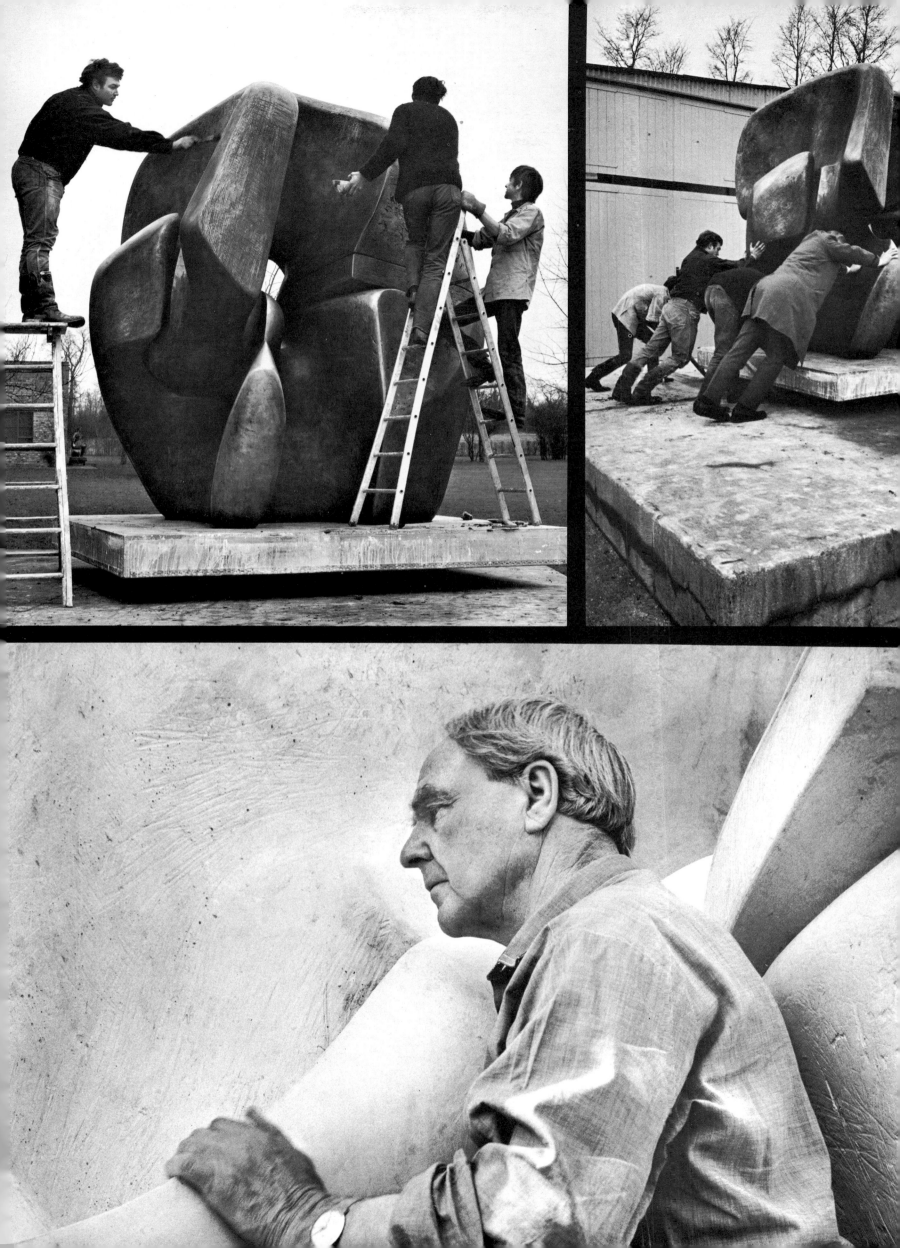

The small version of this piece was originally called "Head in Hand", the hand being the piece at the back. When I came to make it in full size, about eighteen inches high, I gave it a pale golden patina so that each piece reflected a strange, almost ghostly, light at the other. This happened quite by accident. It was because the whole effect reminded me so strongly of the light and shape of the full moon that I have since called it "Moon Head".

"Three Rings", in soraya travertine, is another "fitting-together" sculpture. Although the pieces do not touch, they are articulated like a snake.

"Nuclear Energy", originally "Atom Piece". The title was changed because it was felt that some people might think that the word "piece" meant peace.

I get depressed when I am not working enough. In fact, work is a way of not becoming depressed. Of course there are times when I am disappointed at not achieving some particular aim. But I don't accept, for instance, the general idea that artists are unhappy people. They may be dissatisfied with what they do, but as long as they are creating, they are luckier than people who are just doing humdrum, everyday jobs. I think that, if you can concentrate on work, it is a terrific recompense, a terrific reward in life. To be obsessed with some vision and to have the continuous opportunity of working to realise that vision could be looked upon as God's greatest gift to anyone.

When I was offered the site near the House of Lords for the "Two-Piece Knife Edge" sculpture, I liked the place so much that I didn't bother to go and see an alternative site in Hyde Park. I remembered as a young student, a sculpture called "Rima" by Epstein, a memorial to the poet W. H. Hudson. At the time this work caused a tremendous fuss. I demonstrated with a crowd of students against the general Philistine public, who hated it. It was tarred and feathered and goodness knows what. Six years ago I couldn't find it when I wanted to show it to a foreigner, which proves how easily one lonely sculpture can be lost in a large park. The House of Lords site is quite different. It is next to a path where people walk and it has a few seats where they can sit and contemplate it, unlike the placing of the very fine equestrian statue of Charles the First, in Trafalgar Square, which, in order to look at closely and appreciate in detail, you have to risk your life in crossing a maze of traffic.

There was a tremendous storm one night at home in Much Hadham, and the "Two-piece Knife Edge" sculpture was blown over. This gave me the idea of a sculpture that would lie on the ground like a stranded whale.

One of the great points of sculpture is that it can make people see familiar things in a fresh way. So many people only use their eyes for practical purposes. Through their work, painters and sculptors can give people new visual experiences and a fuller understanding of life. By this I mean people are encouraged to see things more profoundly.

486

While I was working on "The Archer" (pages 488–491) which was destined for Toronto, I was asked to paint a backcloth for T. S. Eliot's memorial programme which was to take place on a Sunday evening at the Globe Theatre. Since I could not stop work on the sculpture for a month, it was suggested that "The Archer" would be even better for the purpose than a backcloth.

The original plaster was so heavy that it could not have been moved without cutting it into several pieces, and so I decided to take a plaster cast of it with a skin a quarter of an inch thick, weighing one tenth of the original. Incidentally, that is why there are two plasters of "The Archer".

On the Saturday evening after the theatre had closed, the plaster arrived by road and we just managed to squeeze it through the door with two inches to spare, and on to the stage by the following morning. All the next day we worked on the stage-lighting until we were happy with it.

On the Sunday night, the programme began with an overture, lasting three or four minutes, which had been specially composed by Stravinsky. Then the curtain went up and the sculpture, which I had placed asymmetrically on the stage and had left its natural white colour, very slowly made one complete revolution in silence. Throughout the evening while Laurence Olivier, Paul Scofield and many others read extracts from Eliot's poetry, we changed the position and the lighting of the sculpture.

It was my first experiment in using real sculpture on the stage instead of fake pictorial scenery, and it was a moving experience. If I ever worked for the theatre again I think, I would use real three-dimensional sculpture and not a pictorial illusion. I am sure there is a future use for real sculpture in the theatre.

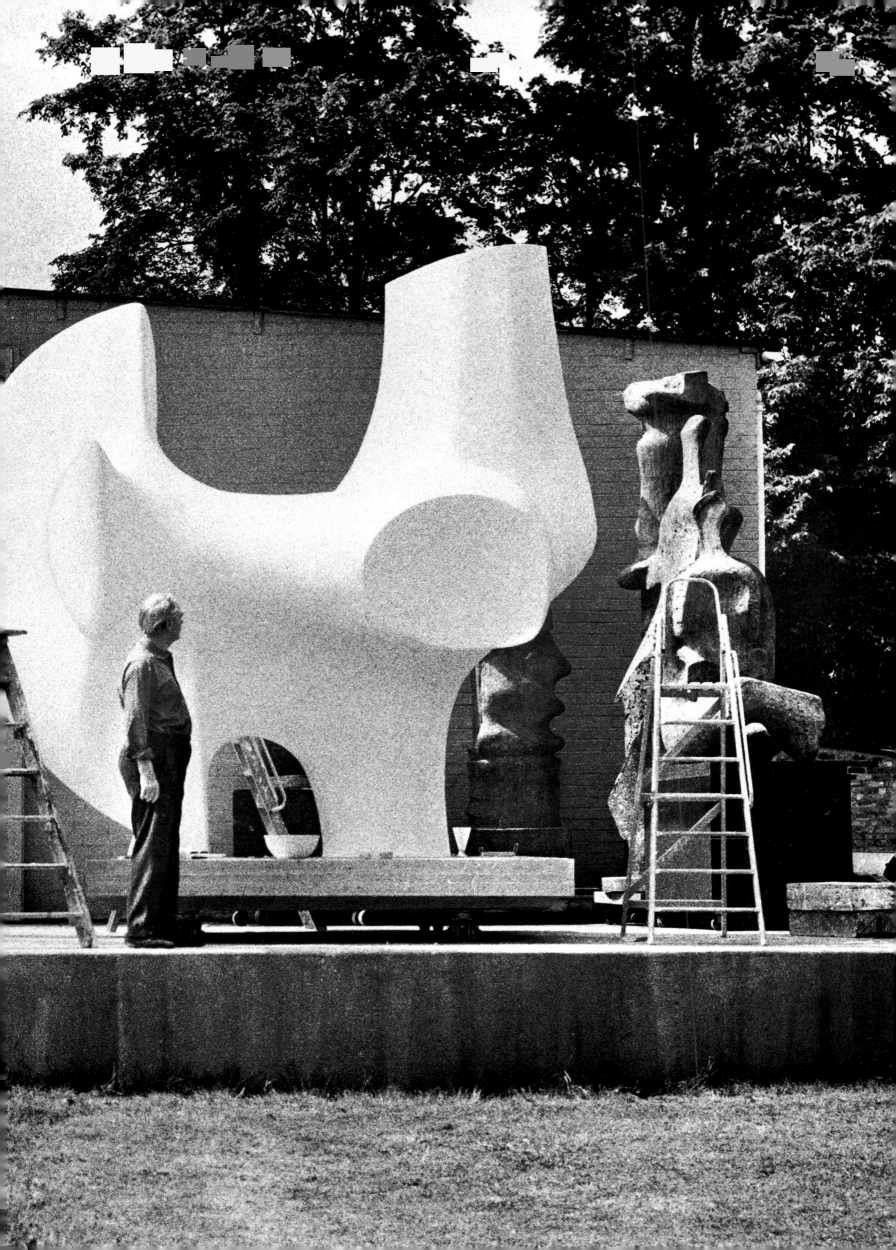

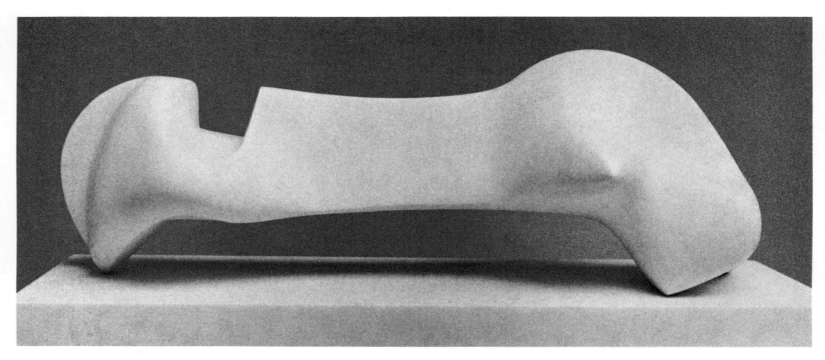

In stone sculpture you have to alter the malleable softness of flesh and blood into something that is harder and less bendable.

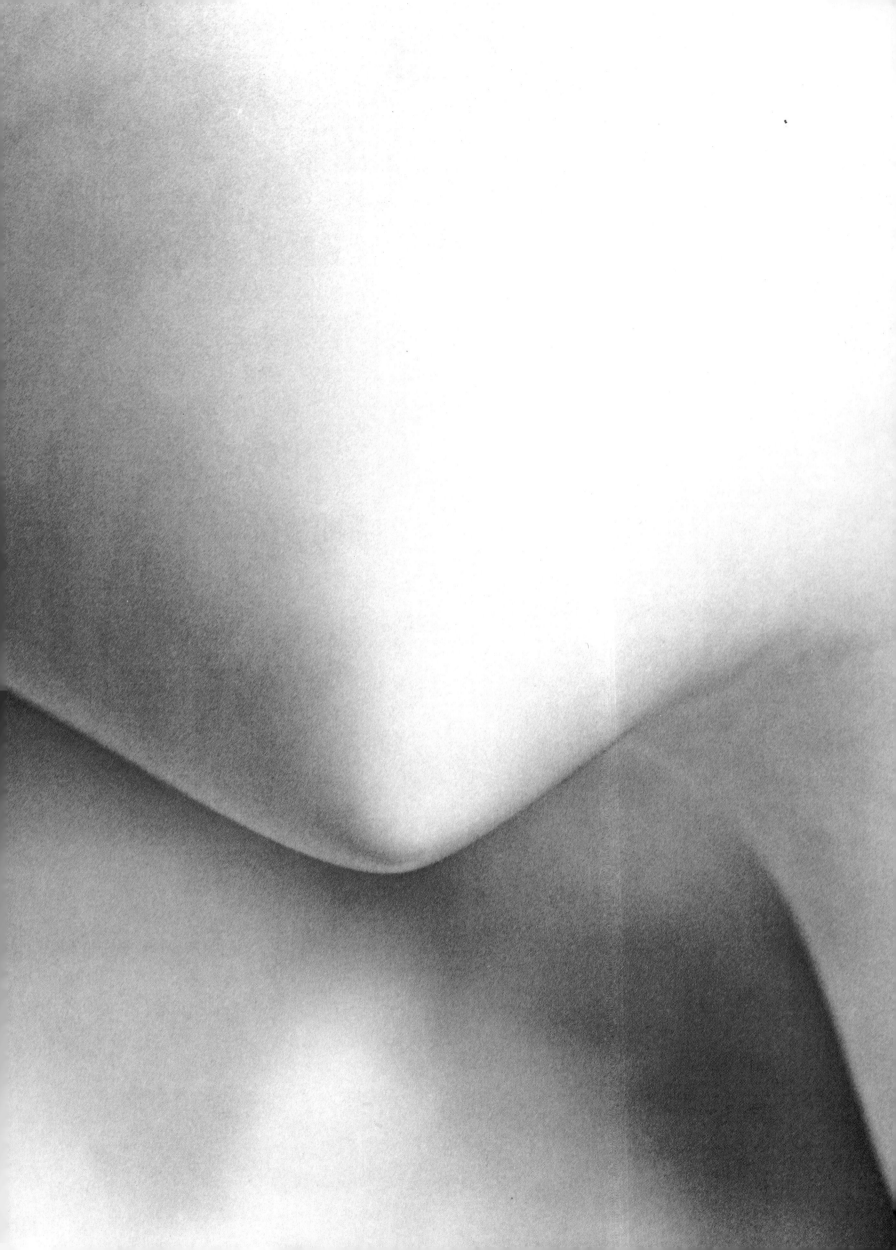

White marble is a most pure and elegant material. In carving a sculpture, it is very important to match the right material with the particular subject in mind. In using white marble I give the forms a precision and refinement and a surface finish that I wouldn't try to obtain with a rough textured stone such as travertine.

1/2/3

4/5/6

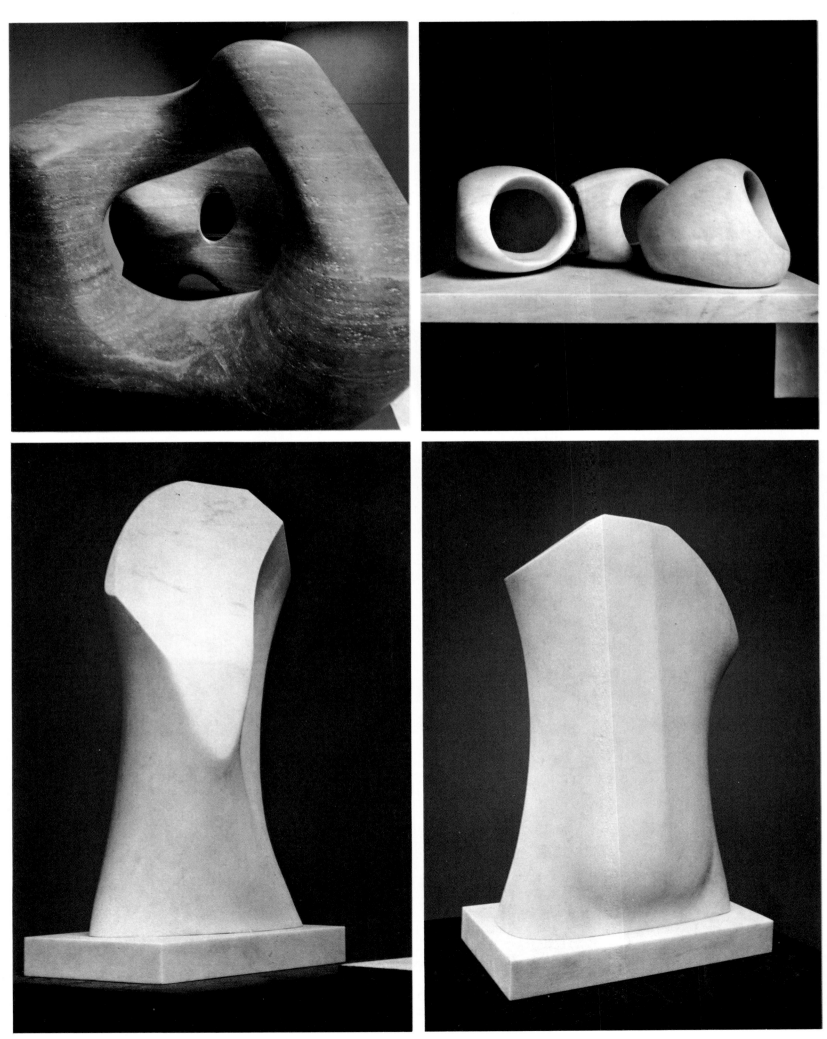

My little studio is a very important "habitat" for me. It is where I am most personally isolated, and that's probably why I like it so much. There are some days when everything I have done in it seems useless or pointless. But this never worries me, because, if a sculpture is eventually going to take up to four months to do, I want to feel that it will be worthwhile. Similarly, if something only takes up two or three hours, it may seem fine at the time but, a month or so later, I might not like it as much. As a result I like my maquettes to survive some test of time before I realise them in their ultimate size.

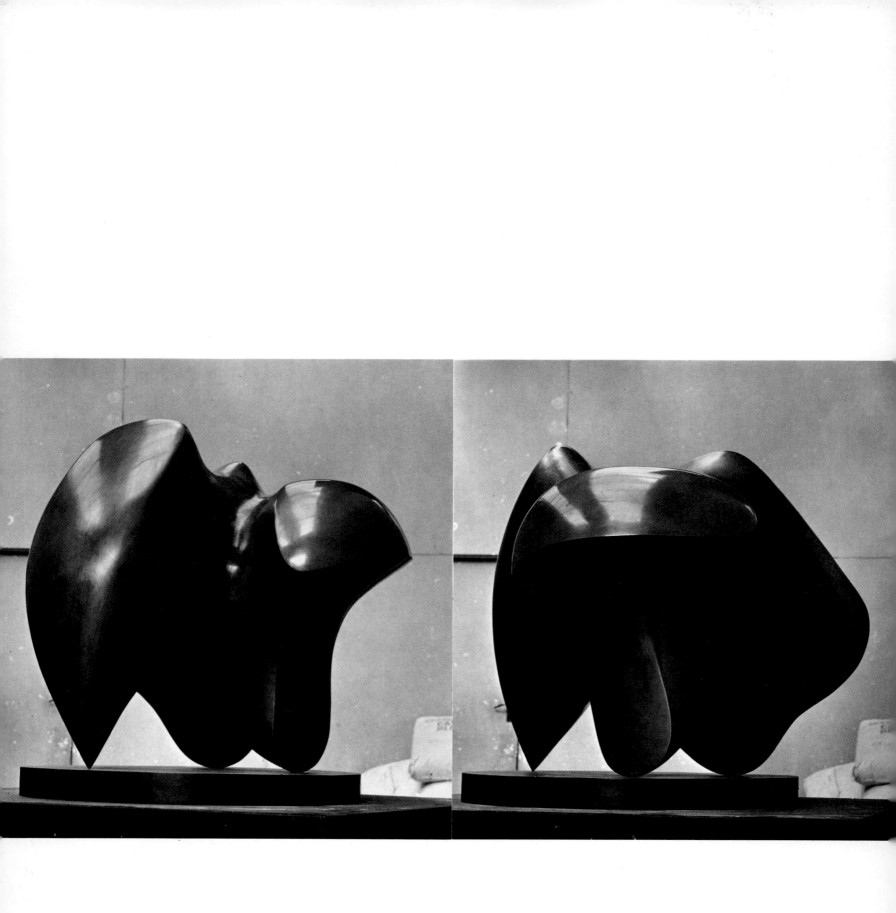

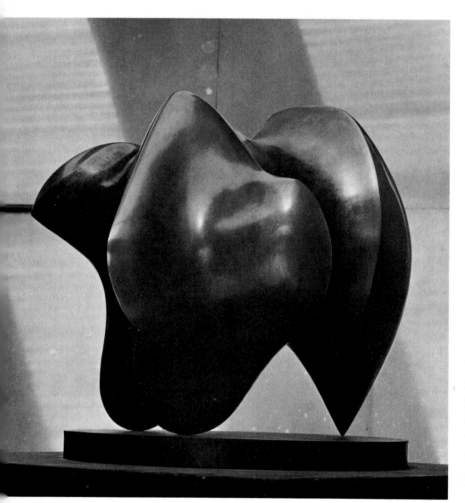

"Three-Way Sculpture: Points" was an attempt to show one work from below as well as from on top and from the side. My idea was to make a new kind of sculpture, less dependent on gravity, which could be seen in at least three positions and be effective in all of them; a sculpture which you could understand more completely because you knew it better. This worked in the maquette, but I made the finished bronze sculpture too large and heavy to be turned over by one person. We all make mistakes.

The variety of objects in my small studio provides me with many new ideas simply by looking at and handling them. This might not happen if each object was in isolation.

1

I call this sculpture "Two-piece: Pipe". It is an attempt to
make a sculpture which is varied in all its views and forms.
One piece is very different from the other, and by combining
the two I obtain many permutations and combinations. By
adding two pieces together the differences are not simply
doubled. As in mathematics, they are geometrically
multiplied, producing an infinite variety of viewpoints.

When Mary was young I would
model or make a little horse for
her to encourage her to do
something. This owl was done
on such an occasion.

I call this sculpture "Ear Piece", because while making it I
was reminded of the human ear. Our ears are remarkable
inventions and can be looked at as sculptures in themselves.
I'm sure that if we had never seen the human ear, if Nature
had just put a hole in its place, it would have been incredible
for man himself to have created so weird a shape.

4

505

I'm not a natural collector myself. It is Irina who is the born collector—from stamps, cacti and pottery to pictures. Except for collecting objects which help me in my work, I am content to go to museums to see works of art, without owning them. We have some examples of primitive art, and lots of "found objects" which give me great pleasure. We also have work by Rodin, Courbet and Seurat, but my most interesting possession is Cézanne's "Bathers".

H.M. with Marino Marini
at Forte dei Marmi
1964.

Photograph taken during a weekend
spent at Stratford on Avon with the
Priestleys.   All five north country men
from left to right —
Fred Hoyle — J.B. Priestley, C. Washbrook
H.M. and Leonard Hutton.

After Honorary Degree Ceremony
at Reading University.
MAY 1959

After Honorary Degree Ceremony
at York University. 1963.

After Honorary Degree
Ceremony at Oxford
University June 1961.
H.M. with fellow Honorand Dame
Peggy Ashcroft.

510

Harry Fischer and Herman Noack.
(my dealer.)   (my Bronze Founder.)
        outside the studio - Much Hadham. 1967.

Portrait
of H.M.
by.
Marini.
1964.

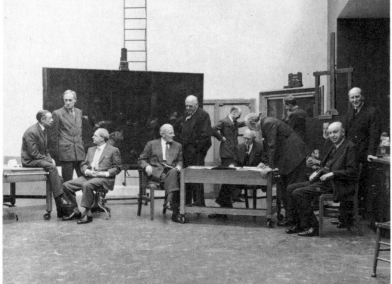

Group picture of National Gallery Trustees
        Photograph taken by Douglas Glass.   1960.

I built this open-air studio of plastic for the Lincoln
Center sculpture, intending to remove it afterwards. Now,
not only have I come to accept it, but I also find it most
useful. It means that I can make large sculptures in natural
light and can see them from all around at all times.
Without this studio several of my larger more recent
sculptures such as "Nuclear Energy", "Two-Piece Knife
Edge" and "Double Oval" could never have been made.
Some people ask me why I live and work in the country.
Space, light and distance are three good reasons.

"Double Oval" is of such a physical size that it evokes
architecture as well as sculpture in its construction. The
two ovals look the same but they are not. Instead they are
echoes of each other.

It is impossible to cast a large sculpture in one piece, for the simple reason that you can only melt a certain amount of bronze in one crucible. Therefore it has to be sawn up into sections, which are cast separately and then welded together. In the case of "Double Oval", Hermann Noack, my bronze-founder from West Berlin, came over to cut the sculpture in the right places.

"Man", who sits alone at the end of my garden, provides a poignant though triumphant end to this book. He began as a detail from the Tate "Family Group". Later, after making a few alterations, I used him as an experiment in casting in concrete. I found the material rather unsympathetic and so I faked him to look like bronze. The only people who were taken in were some local gypsies, who one night rolled all fifteen hundredweight of him a good hundred yards to the fence before one, more suspicious than the rest, struck him with a hammer and discovered not scrap metal but concrete. As I have said so often you should never judge sculpture at first sight.

Catalogue of Sculptures

Acknowledgements

I would first like to thank Henry Moore for his constant
help and encouragement since, as an art student, I first
went to see him at Much Hadham fifteen years ago, and
for the complete freedom he has given me to visit him
on so many occasions ever since.

Needless to say, this book would have been impossible
without his tireless co-operation, although I doubt if he
ever dreamt how much he was letting himself in for when
he became involved with it. Let it suffice to say that he
willingly gave up fourteen Sunday mornings to
tape-recording his comments and at least ten full days
helping us to edit them.

Secondly I must thank my wife Julia, who, as a fellow art
student, introduced me to Henry Moore and who has been
a great source of strength throughout the preparation of
this book.

I am also immensely grateful to Jocelyn Stevens, who
edited the tape recordings, very often into the early hours
of the morning both in London and at Much Hadham, and
who provided many useful suggestions in making this
book.

Among all the many people who have helped me, I mention
in particular Roger Bounds, my assistant at *Queen*
magazine for the last eight years, who was responsible for
printing all the photographs; Wendy Meredith, my
secretary at the Royal College of Art, who in her spare
time transcribed the tape recordings; Sue Collins, Jocelyn
Stevens' assistant, who typed the text in all its later stages;
the Royal College of Art for allowing me to reproduce
Henry Moore's student report; Mrs Betty Tinsley, Henry
Moore's secretary, for searching out the old photographs
which I have very kindly been allowed to use, and for
checking all the descriptions and dates of the sculptures
included in this book; Thomas Nelson, the publishers, for
allowing me to produce a book twice the size they originally
asked for, and Nick Jenkins for all his skill and
enthusiasm in its layout and design.

Public Collections

AUSTRALIA
Adelaide, National Gallery of South Australia
Melbourne, National Gallery of Victoria
Perth, National Gallery of Western Australia
Sydney, National Gallery of New South Wales

AUSTRIA
Vienna, Museum des 20. Jahrhunderts

BELGIUM
Antwerp, Middelheim Park
Brussels, Musée Royale des Beaux-Arts

BRAZIL
Rio de Janeiro, Museo de Arte Moderna

CANADA
Montreal, Museum of Fine Arts
Ottawa, National Gallery of Canada
Toronto, Art Gallery
Toronto, Nathan Phillips Square
Vancouver, Queen Elizabeth Park
Winnipeg, Art Gallery

DENMARK
Humlebaek, Louisiana Museum

EIRE
Dublin, Gallery of Modern Art
Dublin, St. Stephen's Green

FRANCE
Paris, Musée Nationale d'Art Moderne
Paris, UNESCO

GERMANY
Berlin, Akademie der Künste
Berlin, Galerie des 20. Jahrhunderts
Berlin, Opera House
Bochum, Städtische Kunstgalerie
Cologne, City of
Duisburg, Lehmbruck Museum
Essen, Folkwang Museum
Essen, City of
Freiburg-im-Breisgau, University
Frankfurt-am-Main, Opera House
Hamburg, Kunsthalle
Hanover, Niedersächsische Landesgalerie
Hanover, Städtische Galerie
Heidelberg, University
Mannheim, Kunsthalle
Munich, Bayerische Staatsgemäldesammlungen (Neue
Staatsgalerie)
Recklinghausen, Staedtische Kunsthalle
Stuttgart, Federal Parliament, State of Baden-
Württemberg
Wuppertal, City of

GREAT BRITAIN
Aberdeen, City Art Gallery
Bedford, Cecil Higgins Museum
Birmingham, City Art Gallery
Bolton, City Museum and Art Gallery
Cambridge, Clare College
Cambridge, Corpus Christi College
Cambridge, Fitzwilliam Museum
Cambridge, Jesus College
Cardiff, National Museum of Wales
Chichester (Sussex). Bishop Otter College
Claydon (Suffolk), St Peter's Church
Dartington Hall (Devon)
Edinburgh, National Gallery of Scotland
Harlow, Harlow Arts Trust
Huddersfield, City Art Gallery
Hull, Ferens Art Gallery
Leeds, City Art Gallery
Leicester, City Art Gallery
Leicestershire Education Committee
Liverpool, Walker Art Gallery
London, Abingdon Street, Westminster
London, Arts Council of Great Britain
London, British Council
London, Tate Gallery
London, Victoria and Albert Museum
London, Battersea Park (London County Council)
London, Bond Street, Time-Life Building
London, Chelsea School of Art (London County
Council)
London, St James's, London Transport Headquarters
London, Southwark, Brandon Estate (London County
Council)
London, Stepney, Stifford Estate, Clive Street (London
County Council)
Manchester, City Art Gallery
Manchester, Whitworth Art Gallery
Newcastle-on-Tyne, Laing Art Gallery
Northampton, St Matthew's Church
Oxford, Worcester College
Poole (Dorset), Poole College
Stevenage, Barclay School (Hertfordshire Education
Committee)
Wakefield, City Art Gallery

HOLLAND
Amsterdam, Stedelijk Museum
Arnhem, City of
The Hague, Gemeente Museum
Otterlo, Kröller-Müller Museum
Rotterdam, Bouwcentrum
Rotterdam, Boymans-van-Beuningen Museum

ISRAEL
Jerusalem, Hebrew University
Tel Aviv, Museum

ITALY
Rome, Galleria Nazionale d'Arte Moderna
Venice, Galleria d'Arte Moderna

MEXICO
Mexico City, Direcion de Bellas Artes

NEW ZEALAND
Auckland, City Art Gallery

SPAIN
Madrid, Museo Nacional de Arte Moderno

SWEDEN
Gothenburg (Göteborg), City of
Gothenburg (Göteborg), Konstmuseum

SWITZERLAND
Basel, Kunstmuseum
Zollikon-Zürich, Municipality
Zürich, Kunsthaus

UNITED STATES
Atlanta, Art Museum
Blanden (Iowa), Memorial Gallery
Bloomfield Hills (Michigan), Cranbrook Academy of
Art
Boston, Museum of Fine Arts
Boston, University
Buffalo, Albright-Knox Art Gallery
Cambridge (Mass.), Harvard University (Fogg Art
Museum)
Chicago, Art Institute
Chicago University
Cleveland, Museum of Fine Art
Columbia University
Dallas, Museum of Fine Arts
Des Moines (Iowa), Art Center
Detroit, Institute of Arts
Fort Worth (Texas). Amon Carter Museum of Western
Art
Honolulu, Academy of Arts
Ithaca (N.Y.), Cornell University (White Art Museum)
Michigan, University of
Milwaukee, Art Center
Minneapolis, Institute of Arts
Minneapolis, Walker Art Center
New Haven, Yale University Art Gallery
New York, Museum of Modern Art
New York, Solomon R. Guggenheim Museum
New York, Time-Life Building
Northampton (Mass.), Smith College Museum of Art
Pittsburgh, Carnegie Institute
Poughkeepsie (N.Y.), Vasser College
Providence, Rhode Island School of Design
Richmond (Virginia), Museum of Fine Arts
Rochester (N.Y.), University
St Louis, Lambert Airport
St Louis, City Art Museum
St Louis, Washington University
San Francisco, Museum of Art
Toledo (Ohio), Museum of Art
Washington (D.C.), Phillips Memorial Gallery

VENEZUELA
Caracas, Museo de Bellas Artes

Printed in the Netherlands by L. Van Leer & Co. N.V.

Designed by Nicholas Jenkins